WORKING WITHIN DIVERSITY

T0385162

of related interest

Therapy in Colour
Intersectional, Anti-Racist and Intercultural
Approaches by Therapists of Colour
Eds. Mckenzie-Mavinga, Black, Carberry and Ellis
ISBN 978 1 83997 570 7
eISBN 978 1 83997 571 4

Being White in the Helping Professions
Developing Effective Intercultural Awareness
Judy Ryde
Foreword by Colin Lago
ISBN 978 1 84310 936 5
eISBN 978 1 84642 730 5

**Working with Ethnicity, Race and
Culture in Mental Health**
A Handbook for Practitioners
Hári Sewell
Foreword by Suman Fernando
ISBN 978 1 84310 621 0
eISBN 978 1 84642 855 5

Overcoming Everyday Racism
Building Resilience and Wellbeing in the Face
of Discrimination and Microaggressions
Susan Cousins
ISBN 978 1 78592 850 5
eISBN 978 1 78592 851 2

WORKING
WITHIN
DIVERSITY

A Reflective Guide to Anti-Oppressive
Practice in Counselling and Therapy

Myira Khan

Jessica Kingsley Publishers
London and Philadelphia

First published in Great Britain in 2023 by Jessica Kingsley Publishers
An imprint of John Murray Press

4

Copyright © Myira Khan 2023

A CIP catalogue record for this title is available from the British Library
and the Library of Congress

ISBN 978 1 83997 098 6
eISBN 978 1 83997 099 3

Printed and bound in Great Britain by Bell & Bain Limited

Jessica Kingsley Publishers' policy is to use papers that are natural,
renewable and recyclable products and made from wood grown
in sustainable forests. The logging and manufacturing processes
are expected to conform to the environmental regulations
of the country of origin.

Jessica Kingsley Publishers
Carmelite House
50 Victoria Embankment
London EC4Y 0DZ

www.jkp.com

John Murray Press
Part of Hodder & Stoughton Limited
An Hachette UK Company

Dedicated to my mother for her endless support and to my late father for his unwavering belief in me.

Contents

Introduction

About me

Hi, I'm Myira. It is pronounced Myra and the 'i' is silent. This is something I often find myself saying when I introduce myself. My name, its spelling and pronunciation are important to me, because it's my initial introduction to everyone I meet (including you, the reader of this book), and it is a consistent identity factor in being in relationship with me, in being in relationship with Myira. It's how people (you) will remember me and know what to call me, how to identify me and who they (you) are in relationship with. My name is my personalized identity label.

Attached to my name is the rest of my identity. I describe my (intersectional) identity as a hijab-wearing, visibly Muslim, ethnically minoritized Brown, of East-African Asian heritage, English-speaking, higher-degree educated, self-employed woman.

These are some of my valued and treasured aspects of my identity for me, with each identity characteristic reflecting who I feel I am and my experiences and place in the world – my own sense of self, of what makes me 'me'. It's interesting to note that many of them are also dominant visible characteristics of my identity, which have vastly influenced my lived experiences in the world and all my relationships. My identity, particularly my visible identity, has been profoundly influential in my experience as a trainee and qualified counsellor and my experience of delivering training as a counsellor. This has fundamentally shaped my clinical experience and professional development, of which one major outcome has been this book.

About my experience of 'diversity' training

During my own counselling training and placement, I was the only visible Muslim and only ethnically minoritized woman on the course and in my placement organization, which gave me a stark feeling of standing out, being the 'odd one out' and feeling 'different' from everyone else. My faith, ethnicity, gender and age, all dominant identity characteristics, were visible. It was not until the second year of my diploma course that I met other Muslim and ethnically minoritized counsellors when I attended a counselling conference in London. It was a feeling of being 'the only one' until that moment.

My experience of 'difference and diversity' training consisted of only one day on my two-year diploma course and yet that one day has had an impact on my journey and work as a counsellor way beyond what was intended.

Imagine being the only ethnically minoritized and Muslim trainee on the course. You are about to cover 'difference and diversity' on the course. This is *the* lesson on the topic across the entire curriculum. The classroom is set up for us to watch a video of a counselling session that is meant to demonstrate 'working with difference and diversity'. The video starts to play and what becomes immediately apparent is that the counsellor is a white, middle-aged, middle-class man. The client is a visibly Muslim ethnically minoritized woman. This is what was being demonstrated and taught as 'working with difference and diversity'. However, in that moment *I* was identifying with the client. *I* was that 'difference'. I was not the counsellor. I was the 'other'. In that moment, the penny dropped that to be of a minoritized identity is to be seen, positioned, identified and related to as the 'other' and to only be able to be seen and positioned as the client. It also positioned the counsellor, a white middle-aged, middle-class male, as normative, with no acknowledgment of the counsellor's identity or the impact of their identity on the therapeutic relationship or process.

So how could I, as the visible Muslim ethnically minoritized woman, be both counsellor and 'different' at the same time? It seemed that the two were mutually exclusive. It was presented as if in my visible identity, I couldn't be the counsellor, only the client. My identity could only be one or the other – either a counsellor or, if from a minoritized identity, a client. How was I able to hold both? And, more importantly, how could I challenge the narrative that I could be both?

The positioning of culture, race, ethnicity and faith, if not white and European, not only placed everyone else as the 'other' but they were missing in the room as part of the counsellor's identity. Therefore my identity wasn't being acknowledged nor being fully thought about in my training and how I work with my identity and my client's identity in the therapeutic room.

It was from my training experience that my journey began to challenge how 'difference and diversity' are taught on training courses, with their oppressive dynamic of 'othering' (which I will discuss and unpick further in the next chapter) and their mutual exclusivity between the identity of 'counsellor' and being minoritized. This also prompted me to start creating and delivering my own training and workshops on diversity. From this experience, Working within Diversity as an anti-oppressive approach and model emerged.

Gender and sexuality, as part of identity, were being thought about and taught, but why were culture, ethnicity, race and faith not being thought about and taught? I have often heard from fellow tutors – when I discuss this question with them or equally when I'm invited in as a guest tutor to deliver 'diversity' or 'cross-cultural' training and workshops – that many tutors do not have the resources, skills, knowledge or experience to teach diversity confidently nor the confidence to hold and contain the conversations when trainees want to discuss these topics. There is a hesitancy to broach subjects on racism, prejudice or 'difference' for fear of what might happen in the room.

In the feedback from my workshops, counsellors spoke of their original training, where they felt the topic was never fully explored and this was why they were accessing and engaging in the material now as part of their continuing professional development (CPD). They felt that it was the responsibility of the practitioner to independently learn about this topic and fill in the gap which was missing from their core training.

Drawing on my own training experiences, this book focuses on diversity, identity and anti-oppressive practice at its core, with an emphasis on culture, race, ethnicity and faith. This is not to exclude or minimize any other aspect of identity. There are many other books that do a great job of deep-diving into specific identity characteristics such as gender, sexuality, neurodiversity, language, disability and class, within the context of counselling and therapy.

How Working within Diversity emerged from my clinical practice

I first coined the concept 'Working within Diversity' in September 2020, where it was first publicly presented at a workshop on 'working with minoritized clients in counselling'. The Working within Diversity model and approach is a brand-new, anti-oppressive practice for counselling, supervision and all therapeutic practice. For the first time, the Working within Diversity five-component model and approach to anti-oppressive practice is fully set out in this book. It is a culmination of my more than 13 years of clinical practice as a counsellor, supervisor and counselling tutor, and the many workshops and courses I have delivered on the topics of diversity, culture and identity over the last seven years.

From the feedback I have received from many workshop and course delegates and training institutions over the years, I have been so pleased to discover that many counselling services, counsellors, therapists and training organizations are open to learning about the theme of diversity and its connected concepts of intersectionality, identity, power and anti-oppressive practice in therapeutic spaces, relationships and processes.

The feedback identified four key areas of new growth, learning and development for counsellors, supervisors and therapeutic practitioners in their understanding and application of diversity, culture, identity and intersectionality in therapeutic/supervision practice.

1. Concepts of diversity and identity: rethinking what the concepts mean; what to consider when thinking of these concepts; developing broader thinking and learning new perspectives on these concepts within a safe learning environment; how individuals relate to their own sense of identity; recognizing that there are two identities in the therapeutic process and relationship.
2. Therapist/supervisor's identity: acknowledging the impact of the therapist/supervisor's identity on the therapeutic/supervision process and relationship; therapists/supervisors being able to acknowledge more of their own self and identity and the impact on therapeutic process and relationships; therapists/supervisors recognizing their own values and beliefs and the impact of these on their practice and how they present and show up in the therapeutic space.
3. Clinical/therapeutic practice: applying Working within Diversity in clinical/therapeutic practice; being open to and bringing in new understanding of and insights to clinical/therapeutic practice; what needs to change to offer anti-oppressive practice; developing greater insight and deeper reflexive practice in counselling and supervision; recognizing and working with external 'out there' contexts in the 'in here' therapeutic space.
4. Therapeutic process: therapists/supervisors being able to explore identity and work within diversity; seeing diversity as the context of their shared therapeutic space rather than as the 'other'/client; working 'with' diversity.

The feedback highlighted the lack of training on this topic in our core training programmes and the need for commitment to ongoing development, for creating safe spaces to learn, understand and discuss these topics, for having the space to think about our own identity within relationships and for acknowledging the importance of these topics and learning about their significance and place within counselling. I hope that this book offers you a safe space to think and reflect on these important topics, in a manner that supports your development and ongoing learning about their significance and central place within counselling, therapeutic and supervision practice.

The context for the Working within Diversity model

The Working within Diversity model transcends therapeutic modalities as it identifies how we work within therapeutic relationships to acknowledge and account for the unique identity and individuality of both counsellor and client. It acknowledges and identifies how both experience the work because of their two identities, how they can make sense of what the client brings into the room because of the client's unique identity and experience in the world, alongside acknowledging and understanding that the unique therapeutic relationship is created between and because of the two identities.

We are acknowledging that both people in the therapeutic relationship hold their own unique worldview and experience because of their identity. We, as counsellors, are working beyond our identity, culture and worldview and within the diversity of differing identities, cultures, worldviews and lived experiences.

It feels as if conversations about the power, privilege, biases and projections that exist in the counselling and psychotherapy profession are needed now more than ever. The Black Lives Matter movement, the murder of George Floyd and the spotlight on intersectionality, power and privilege in recent years have pushed these issues into the foreground. These issues are all connected to the counselling and therapy profession and clinical work we engage in.

It is imperative that we understand systemic, structural, social, political, cultural, historical, societal, community and familial contexts when working as counsellors, because they are right there in the room with us. They are right there in the truth (identity, narrative and lived experiences) of our clients. They are right there in our own truth (our own identity, narrative and lived experiences).

Everything about what happens in the world is evidence that counselling is an act of social justice. We can't hold the truth of our clients without acknowledging and understanding the existence and impact of social, structural and systemic inequalities in the world.

We must recognize and understand that:

- counselling is an act of social justice
- therapy is political
- therapy is cultural
- therapy is social
- therapy is politically, culturally, socially, structurally and systemically located.

Our identity, intersectionality and experiences of holding power and privilege, and our experiences of being oppressed, marginalized and minoritized, are core elements to our everyday lived experiences. They are not afterthoughts to how we experience the world, how we understand and reflect on the ways in which we experience the world or how the world treats us in return. Therefore, they can't be afterthoughts in our counselling training and practice, in how we understand our relationship between ourselves, our identity and the world, how we relate to our clients, how we establish our therapeutic relationships, how we work with our clients and how we can understand what is happening in our therapeutic relationships and why.

We need to acknowledge our clients' lived experiences of power, privilege and oppression. To be blind to structural and systemic inequality is to be blind to our client's truth. To acknowledge the oppression, power, privilege and structural inequalities experienced by clients 'out there' in the world, is to also acknowledge how they are experienced 'in here', in the therapy room, in our therapeutic relationships and in our therapeutic process and culture.

Truth is a person's identity, narrative and lived experiences, and I am always mindful of our ability to hold, contain, value and respect the truth of our clients – and that each client's truth doesn't diminish or erase our own truth in any way. It's about our ability to mutually honour two truths in the therapy room at the same time: the truth of our client and our own truth.

This book is an invitation to start understanding intersectionality, identity, culture and diversity in therapeutic practice and relationships, and to explore how you and your identity as a counsellor/practitioner and a client's identity impact on and influence your therapeutic relationship. Who you are has an influence over the experience and interaction with your clients, and we must always keep in mind that the relationship between two people – two identities – is always at play in every therapeutic relationship and is always impacting on the process. Who we are as counsellors/practitioners – our identity – is an active aspect. No longer are we the blank slate, the invisible counsellor, the neutral person in this therapeutic process. We are a proactive part of the work, of the relationship, of the process, having influence and holding power in, on and over the work.

Working within Diversity is a two-fold commitment: first to anti-oppressive activism, by acknowledging and challenging the structural and systemic inequalities of society, and second to anti-oppressive practice, by making sure we understand how and why those same structural and systemic inequalities and power dynamics are present 'in here' and what we can do so that they don't unconsciously, intentionally/unintentionally or automatically get repeated 'in here'. Instead of re-creating oppression we must instead create anti-oppressive practice and relationships to flatten the power between counsellor and client, or supervisor and supervisee.

A note on applying the Working within Diversity model to couples counselling and group therapy

While the book has explicitly set out the model and its application to individual counselling and supervision, the approach is equally applicable to working with couples and groups. Where we address working in therapeutic relationship with one client, we can substitute this for working with a couple or multiple clients. Where we practise the principle of 'two truths' – that in any therapeutic relationship we sit with our own truth and our client's truth – in couples work we sit with 'three truths' (each person's truth in the room) and in groups we sit with the number of truths as there are people present, as we are holding the identity, narrative and lived experiences of each person in mind.

How to use the book

This is a reflective guide for anyone engaging in therapeutic practice. This includes counsellors, therapists and psychologists, alongside mental health support workers, well-being practitioners, mental health first aiders, chaplains, therapeutic coaches and anyone who offers a therapeutic service to others.

This guide is an experience we'll walk through together. I'm not here standing at the front of a lecture theatre and bombarding you with lots of content, without a chance to think, reflect and apply what this means for you in your clinical/ therapeutic practice. That would be oppressive in itself!

Instead, this book is an opportunity to take the time to reflect on your own identity. I'm offering you plenty of reflective opportunities and spaces throughout the book to note your thoughts and reflections on the issues, what comes up for you and how the topics may be applied or reflected on in relation to your clinical work. These spaces are clearly marked as 'reflective exercises'.

I will be walking you through these reflective exercises throughout the book to address how to work within diversity and since this involves you, your identity and your lived experiences, I am inviting you to be honest and open with yourself about your experiences personally, professionally and clinically/therapeutically. This will support your understanding of how you currently work with clients, how you establish, manage and make sense of your therapeutic relationships and what is happening in the counselling room. These exercises will also support you to understand how you can start to work within diversity and apply the learning from this book in your clinical/therapeutic practice, to start an anti-oppressive practice, and work within the rich diversity of you and your clients' truths. This workbook will be useful to you depending on the degree you want to engage in and commit to the content and material in your own reflexivity and reflective process, as well as how you want to apply your reflections, learning and growth to your clinical/therapeutic practice.

Where any template has been used, as part of the reflective process or in a reflective exercise, an additional blank version of the template has been included in the Appendix for your use. The Appendix is available to download online at https://library.jkp.com/redeem using the voucher code FTHRMFA.

The chapters are sequenced, but if you imagine the book as a map and the chapters as regions on the map, the map and its regions illustrate the landscape of anti-oppressive practice and 'working within diversity', which we are navigating in our clinical/therapeutic practice. It also means that the order of chapters is not hierarchical (i.e. not oppressive), but instead you are welcome to dip in and out of the chapters in any order, as if exploring any region of the map you choose to. Just note that if you do dip into the later chapters on therapeutic practice first (in Parts 3 and 4), some of the reflective exercises may reference their earlier related chapters and reflective exercises on understanding the concepts themselves (in Part 2). You may find that participating in these earlier reflective exercises (in Part 2) will help you in getting the most out of the later chapters and reflective exercises on therapeutic practice.

Part 1 (Moving from Working 'with' Diversity to Working within Diversity) explores the current 'working with diversity' concept and introduces the Working within Diversity model and its five components, as the anti-oppressive approach, practice and lens for therapeutic practice.

Part 2 (Exploring Diversity and Identity) explores our understanding of diversity, identity, intersectionality and identity characteristics, and introduces us to the concepts considered within the Working within Diversity model and its five components.

Part 3 (Working within Diversity in Therapeutic Practice) explores the application of the Working within Diversity model to the therapeutic context and outlines how to utilize and apply the five components to therapeutic work, to understand how to offer anti-oppressive practice.

Part 4 (Working within Diversity in Reflective Practice) explores the application of the model and its anti-oppressive approach to supervision, how to develop anti-oppressive supervision and supervisory relations, alongside a reflective approach to thinking about self-care, and how to move forward in your development and growth as an anti-oppressive practitioner.

A note on terminology

I do not make a distinction between counselling and therapy or counsellor and therapist, as they are equally therapeutic practices and titles. Throughout this book, wherever I state 'therapy' or 'counselling', I am referring to and include all therapeutic practices. Wherever I state 'counsellor' or 'therapist', I am referring to and include all therapeutic practitioners.

PART 1

Moving from Working 'with' Diversity to Working within Diversity

In Part 1, I will deconstruct the current 'working with diversity' concept and introduce you to the Working within Diversity model, its five components and seven principles, as an anti-oppressive approach, practice and lens to therapeutic work.

Before we get going, let's find out your starting point, in our first reflective exercises.

Reflective exercises

How do you feel about the concepts of 'difference' and 'diversity'?

....

....

....

....

....

....

....

....

Have you experienced being taught 'difference and diversity' during your counselling/therapy training? Was it a day, or a half-day or module training? What did it look like? How do you feel about the training you received on it (if you did)? How did it impact your clinical practice?

....

....

....

....

....

....

....

What does 'working with diversity' mean to you? What does it look like in your practice or understanding of therapeutic practice?

....

....

....

....

....

....

Where are you currently in your thinking, working and reflecting on 'diversity' and/or 'difference' in your work?

....

....

....

....

....

....

What does anti-oppressive practice mean to you? What do you think it looks like in practice?

....

....

....

....

....

....

As well as reflecting on this now, you will be invited to complete a similar exercise at the end of this book, to reflect on your growth and development throughout the process of working with the material and content presented here. It will enable you to explore the ways in which you have expanded your understanding of diversity and working in an anti-oppressive way with clients or supervisees.

CHAPTER 1

The Problem of 'Working with Diversity and/or Difference'

To be intentional in developing and offering an anti-oppressive practice in therapy and supervision, we need to acknowledge how current practice is oppressive, and we must be clear on what we mean by 'oppression' and 'anti-oppressive'.

> **Oppression:** the systematic targeting of a non-dominant low social status group by a dominant high social status group through their power and prejudice, by marginalizing, discriminating and disempowering the non-dominant group, for the benefit of the dominant group to retain and maintain their systemic and structural power, authority and privilege.

What is anti-oppressive practice?

Anti-oppressive practice explicitly acknowledges structural and systemic inequalities, systems of oppression and the entire power-oppression relational dynamic, whereby social groups are either powerful and privileged (relationally oppressing other groups) at one end of the spectrum or minoritized and marginalized (relationally oppressed by the dominant groups) at the other end of the spectrum. This supports an understanding of how each person is shaped by their lived experiences, by the underlying systemic and structural context of their lived experiences and which end of systems of oppression and power-oppression relational dynamics they experience.

Anti-oppressive practice supports an approach to offer a relational dynamic of equality and flatten the power-oppression hierarchy in our practice, in our processes and our relationships. It identifies the 'out there' context within which clients have their lived experiences of privilege and/or oppression, while also acknowledging the structural inequalities of the 'in here' context and working to even out the power and oppression between counsellor and client. This offers a therapeutic process and relationship that holds the client in equal regard to the practitioner, without the client being marginalized, minoritized or 'othered' by the therapeutic practice or practitioner.

We need to understand that current practice can take an oppressive dynamic and stance, both consciously and unconsciously, both intentionally and unintentionally. One place where this is happening is in the labelling and teaching of 'working with diversity and/or difference'.

The oppressive stance of 'working with diversity and/or difference'

Whenever difference or diversity is taught on counselling or psychotherapy training programmes, how it is usually presented is under the term 'working with diversity and/or difference'.

When broken down, there are five inherent problems with the oppressive term 'working with diversity and/or difference', listed below and then each explained in further detail:

1. The 'bolt-on'
2. Client as 'diverse' and counsellor as 'normative'
3. Counsellor's identity is missing
4. Relational dynamic and power in the therapeutic relationship
5. Unequal weighting on client's identity

1. The 'bolt-on'
The term is problematic because it places 'working with diversity and/or difference' as something separate to the therapeutic relationship, rather than it being part of or considered within the therapeutic relationship. Instead, it is positioned and contextualized as an add on, as an additional concept to think about after we have already thought about the therapeutic relationship. This so often then is reflected in where it gets positioned in the counselling training itself, as a 'bolt-on' part of the teaching, rather than an integral, embedded and integrated aspect of clinical work and the therapeutic relationship. When 'diversity' training is positioned as a bolt-on, it is seen as an addition, unimportant, a tick-box exercise. By having it central and embedded, it can rightly be positioned as a core aspect of empathy and the therapeutic relationship, necessary to understand the truth of our clients.

2. Client as 'diverse' and counsellor as 'normative'

The term 'working with diversity and/or difference' is oppressive in its nature because of how it positions the counsellor and client in relation to each other. We have for too long positioned 'working with diversity and/or difference' training as the identity label. The identity of 'difference' or 'diversity' itself gets projected onto the client. This can only in return label and identify the counsellor as 'normative' or neutral, with the client being 'different' from the normative and centred counsellor.

'Working with' sets up the relational dynamic that the normative counsellor is in relationship with the 'difference' or 'diverse' identity, that being the client. The client, in being labelled as 'diverse' or 'different' from the counsellor, is relationally positioned as the 'other' from the normative centred position of the counsellor, who is seen as belonging to the majority position. This locates 'diversity' in the client's identity and implies that the client's identity is 'diverse', and the client is 'different' from the centred counsellor or normative 'characteristics' of whiteness, middle-class, middle-aged and heterosexual (see Figure 1).

This defines therapeutic relationships as being between a normative, neutral centred counsellor and a 'different' or 'diverse' client, which is problematic for the therapeutic relationship and process, as the counsellor is now working 'with' someone outside their 'norm', someone who is immediately seen as different from them. This is the process of the client being 'othered' by the counsellor.

3. Counsellor's identity is missing

The focus on the client and their 'diverse' or 'different' identity makes no reference to the counsellor's identity or its impact on the therapeutic relationship or process. The identity of the counsellor is essentially missing and doesn't get considered, when looking at the relationship, to understand how and why the dynamic is unfolding in the way it is and how and why the client is relating to the counsellor in the way they are. This denies any influence or impact from the counsellor and places all responsibility and understanding on the client and their identity – it can't be because of the counsellor's identity or who they represent to the client, either consciously or unconsciously.

4. Relational dynamic and power in the therapeutic relationship

'Working with' sets up a conscious and unconscious relational dynamic between the normative counsellor and 'different' client, for which the power differential between the two positions of 'normative' and 'different from the normative' is played out in the relationship.

This positions any client with any characteristic in their identity different from the counsellor as somebody who then becomes the 'other' and by doing so the counsellor immediately positions the client as different from themselves and what is deemed normal or normative. This sets up a relationship dynamic where the counsellor then perceives the client or tries to make sense of the client's world through the counsellor's normative or neutral lens. The counsellor ends up in an observational position with their normative lens.

'Working with diversity' inherently implies a 'diversion' from the normative too, which looks to diversity as an external reflection of clients. It is not 'working within diversity'. It is the privilege and social positioning of practitioners within the profession and training.

This can lead to the client's issues or narrative not always being understood from the client's own lived experience, frame of reference or internal world but instead observed and interpreted through the counsellor's normative lens. When the counsellor positions themselves in this neutral normative position not only is the counsellor's own identity not being taken into consideration but the relationship itself between the client and counsellor is then not being understood as two identities in relationship with one another. Instead, the client's identity is seen as different, and this becomes oppressive in its practice because the client is being seen and related to as if they are a minority or different from the norm or majority and they are then perceived and related to as the other or the outsider. This can unconsciously invite an oppressor-oppressed power dynamic to be played out in the relationship because the counsellor takes up a position of power over the client. In later chapters, we will address how a power dynamic can get played out in therapeutic relationships and why we need to be mindful of conscious and unconscious oppressive practice that gets enacted within the 'in here' counselling space and relationship, and how we move to an equality within the relationship.

5. Unequal weighting on client's identity

Working 'with' only acknowledges one truth (that of the client) with no processing or reflection of how the truth or identity of the counsellor has an impact on the process.

This implies that the counsellor's identity has zero impact on the process – that they are neutral and not a variable factor in the process.

What 'working with difference and diversity' completely fails to acknowledge is that the therapeutic relationship encompasses and contains two people and therefore two identities, two lived experiences, two diversities in relationship with one another. The meeting of those two identities in relationship with one another then creates a unique therapeutic relationship in and of itself and it is this that doesn't get taken into consideration when we position the client as different and diverse from an identity-neutral counsellor.

Figure 1: 'Working with diversity' (relational dynamic)

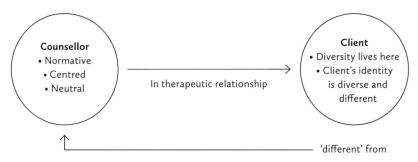

Reflective exercises

What are your thoughts, feelings and reflections on the phrase 'working with diversity'?

....

....

....

....

....

What are your thoughts, reflections or reactions in learning about the critiques of 'working with diversity'? What questions come to mind? What are you curious about or to learn more about?

....

....

....

....

....

....

CHAPTER 2

Working within Diversity –
The Model and Approach

The Working within Diversity model outlines five components to working in an anti-oppressive practice and approach, by offering a map to navigate the landscape of diversity and identity and by placing ourselves on the map and therefore 'within' diversity (see Figure 2).

The five components of the model are:

Component 1: Structural and Systemic Context of Counselling

Component 2: Identity and Intersectionality (of counsellor and client or supervisor and supervisee)

Component 3: Power

Component 4: Therapeutic Relationship (in therapy and supervision)

Component 5: Therapeutic Process (in therapy and supervision)

These five components offer an approach for an anti-oppressive working relationship, between two people. The approach acknowledges the external 'out there' societal contexts of power, privilege and oppression, how these impact on both people's identity, lived experience and experience in relationships, and how they relate to others. It also acknowledges how this may impact and influence how they show up and relate to one another in the 'in here' therapeutic space and relationship.

All five components co-materialize, so they all manifest at the same time. They are also intra-active (they become active between each other) and are in relationship with one another. By co-materializing this has an impact on their intra-activity and vice-versa – that is, by existing at the same time, they are in relationship with one another, and being in relationship with one another influences how they are showing up and existing. So there is a feedback loop between the quality of the components showing up and the quality of relationships between them.

By not privileging one component over another, we are not oppressing the other four components. Instead we are giving equal weight to all five components, so that the model itself is anti-oppressive, by flattening the power or hierarchy between the components and creating equality among them.

Figure 2: Working within Diversity model (with five components of model)

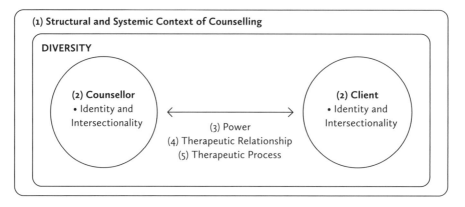

Each of these five components are explained in more depth in Chapters 3–11, before we look at how we can apply these components to therapeutic practice in Chapters 12–19.

The model is built on a set of principles that create the anti-oppressive approach and that will be explained below.

Working within Diversity – an anti-oppressive approach

'Working within diversity' is an approach by which we can develop and ensure anti-oppressive practice in our counselling and therapeutic relationships. This is because 'working within diversity' addresses the previously identified imbalance, bias, problems, faults and relational oppression of 'working with diversity and/or difference'.

The Working within Diversity model uses a set of seven principles as its foundation, which are embedded within the five components.

The seven principles are:

1. Anti-oppressive not inclusive
2. Systemic, structural and social inequalities and oppressions

3. Two identities
4. Two truths
5. Two identities in the therapeutic relationship
6. Culturally attuned
7. Re-establishing external contexts

Each principle is explained in detail below.

Principle 1: Anti-oppressive not inclusive

Anti-oppressive practice is not about 'being inclusive'. On the power-oppressive relational spectrum, being inclusive means to 'other' minoritized communities and groups, while taking up a position yourself as 'normative' and allowing the 'normative' identity to stay invisible. Being inclusive means to include those who are oppressed but still maintain your power by positioning yourselves as normative, neutral, centred and invisible. Inclusive implies that there must be a level of exclusion taking place. Being exclusionary means using your power to put up barriers and having the power, dominance and authority to choose who you include and exclude.

Anti-oppressive practice explicitly acknowledges structural and systemic inequalities, systems of oppression and the entire power-oppression relational dynamic. It acknowledges all identities as visible, without the dominant identity positioned as normative, neutral, centred and invisible. The dynamic is that social groups at one end of the spectrum are powerful and privileged (relationally oppressing other groups) or are being minoritized and marginalized (relationally oppressed by the supremist dominant groups) at the other end of the spectrum. This supports an understanding of how each person is shaped by their lived experiences, by the underlying systemic and structural context of their lived experiences and which end of systems of oppression they experience. This is part of working and being anti-oppressive, and is not the same dynamic of 'inclusion', which doesn't address the systems of oppression or entire power-oppression relational dynamic.

Anti-oppressive practice not only acknowledges systemic and structural inequalities but intentionally works to flatten the power in therapeutic practice, processes and relationships, to hold the client in equal regard to the practitioner and to prevent the client from being marginalized, minoritized or 'othered'.

Principle 2: Systemic, structural and social inequalities and oppressions

To work and deliver anti-oppressive practice is to acknowledge that both current oppressive practice and the profession are born out of and sit within the systemic, structural and social spectrums of power-oppression.

To offer anti-oppressive practice, we need to be honest and courageous enough to ask ourselves how we are currently upholding oppressive practice, oppressing clients or supervisees. How are we sitting in our power and privilege, without acknowledging it or challenging it? How are we reinforcing the power-oppressive relational dynamic within our therapeutic and supervision relationship? How is the profession and its structural frameworks of training, qualifying, practising and building a career setting us up to engage in relationally oppressive dynamics? We must acknowledge that the profession's structure is based on power and hierarchy. So where do we end up and how do we want to challenge ourselves and the profession to develop an anti-oppressive attitude and practice?

We must commit to:

- recognizing and acknowledging the impact of systemic, structural and social inequalities
- recognizing and acknowledging identity and intersectional identities and their impact on people's lived experiences
- recognizing and acknowledging the impact of systems of oppressions and the use of power, privilege and oppression in relational dynamics, which also continue to uphold the supremacy of dominant identity groups and societies
- being proactively involved in anti-oppressive practice, in its development, in our ongoing learning and in its application to our work and profession
- not proactively engaging in oppressive practices, leaving us in the position of passivity, indifference, unawareness or inaction, which reflects a dominant, oppressive attitude and continues to uphold and indicate our support of current systemic inequalities and power-oppressive relational dynamics without challenging them.

In Chapters 6–10, we will be exploring the systemic and structural context in further detail.

Principle 3: Two identities

Moving from 'with diversity' as bolt-on in training to 'working within diversity' acknowledges and embeds into the therapeutic relationship our clear understanding and awareness of there being two people (two identities) in the relationship and both people in a relational dynamic in the space in between them.

'Working within diversity' directly acknowledges there are two unique identities, which are in relationship with one another. It repositions both counsellor and client within their own unique identity and intersectionality. The identity of the client and counsellor are both acknowledged and seen for their own unique diversity and intersectionality and the relationship that then unfolds between the two of them does so because of the two identities and the impact and influence of the two identities relating to one another.

The diversity of the counsellor and the counsellor's identity is in relationship with the diversity of the client and the client's identity. There are no normative, centred or neutral identity factors located with either the counsellor or client. The therapeutic relationship and two identities are all contained within an understanding of 'identity' and a context of 'diversity', whereby all identities are seen as diverse. 'Working within diversity' also acknowledges the historical, ancestral and cultural identities of both people in the relationship and the differences between the identities of the two people in the relationship.

The counsellor's identity is not a blank slate or 'neutral'. The counsellor's identity is present, proactive and of value. It offers a diversity of identity. In the same way, the client's identity is also a diversity of an identity. Both identities are fully present in the room and in the relationship. Our visible identity as the counsellor – our ethnicity, gender, visible faith, age, visible ability or disability – can't be removed, dismissed, ignored or made invisible. Our identity is reacted, related and responded to, consciously and unconsciously by the client. It's how we work with it that matters and that is 'working within diversity'.

Each identity has its own version of what is 'normal' or 'normative' to them. The key is to know that about yourself, that your lens is biased because of your identity, intersectionality, social position and lived experience. Your client does not have the same 'norm' as you. They have their norm, which you need to learn and be able to see the world through their 'norm' lens and worldview.

Understanding yourself is key to understanding others. To know your own culture, identity, intersectionality, lived experiences and experiences of power, privilege and oppression enables you to also know others, and their identity and lived experience in the world. We need to take on and understand the client as a whole, all parts of their identity and lived experiences and sense of self, which includes their past, history, generational legacy, who they are now and their current experiences.

We all carry our internalized lived experiences. This includes our familial, cultural, social and political history, the influence and relationship of our intersectional identity and being socially located on systems of oppression. We need to hold on to the two identities having been formed out of their unique intersectional identities and lived experiences and be able to acknowledge both simultaneously, without them competing with one another, or repeating a power-oppressive relational dynamic.

Principle 4: Two truths
Working 'with' places an unequal weighting and a focus on the client's identity over

everything else, which privileges the client's identity above anything else, marginalizing the rest of the counselling process as well as minoritizing the counsellor, their identity and any impact their identity and presence may have on the client, the therapeutic relationship or therapeutic process.

'Working within diversity' holds all components of the therapeutic process, relationship and both identities of the counsellor and client on an equal weighting. There is no 'privileging' of one factor, component or piece of context over another, which would oppress, marginalize or minimize aspects of the process, relationship or identities.

Truth encompasses a person's identity, narrative and lived experiences. Holding the two identities and two lived experiences in mind, in every therapeutic and supervisory relationship, is to hold the two truths of two people's unique lived experiences and how they have been related to and treated in the world itself. These two truths exist simultaneously in the relationship, in the room and in the process. Sitting with two truths, which possibly conflict or contradict one another, is anti-oppressive itself, as we must be open to sitting with two different experiences, perspectives and worldviews, one our own and one our client's, without wanting to oppress, dismiss, reject, minimize or minoritize the other person's truth – or pathologize their truth, which would lead to further alienation for them.

To work anti-oppressively is to hold both truths, even if they conflict, and to hold and bear the tension of the truths, without oppressing one over the other. We must hold both truths as equally valid. This means to work with, honour, value, empathize and explore the client's truth without wanting to oppress it and to only keep our own truth as valid. In addition, we must not oppress our own truth through our internalized oppression or internalized racism, or dismiss, ignore or deny our own feelings, identity or experiences, so that we are only keeping the client's truth as valid.

Principle 5: Two identities in the therapeutic relationship

Anti-oppressive practice honours two equal identities that engage in the 'in here' space and the therapeutic process and relationship which unfolds. 'Working within diversity' acknowledges both counsellor and client, both of their identities, and encompasses those two identities in relationship with one another, with an understanding that the two identities will impact and influence the relationship itself. It sets up a relationship dynamic between the counsellor and client in which the two identities are considered when understanding what is happening between the two of them within the therapeutic relationship itself.

The therapeutic relationship is the most crucial and determining factor in the efficacy, impact and outcome of counselling. The identity of the counsellor is just as important an influencing factor on the relationship as the identity of the client – both impact the process, quality and efficacy of the therapeutic relationship. Neither the counsellor nor the client is 'neutral' in the relationship – both their identities impact on and influence the relationship being created.

If counselling efficacy is based on the therapeutic relationship, and the two people in that relationship are vital to its outcome, we can't ignore the identity, lived experiences and intersectionality of each person entering that relationship.

When we see so many clients who look for a culturally or faith-matched counsellor, we know that for clients the identity of the counsellor matters and yet we do not address that in our training (from a relational perspective) nor from a dynamic perspective of intersectionality, power-oppression and how the identity of the counsellor may impact on the client and vice-versa. In training, we may acknowledge the power of being a counsellor (our power role) but what of the power in all the other aspects of our identity?

What 'working within diversity' addresses and represents is a repositioning of the relationship dynamic from a counsellor who is normative and a client who is 'different', to both counsellor and client occupying their own unique identity and intersectionality. Therefore the relationship between both counsellor and client is one in which both are working from their own unique identity and the relationship encompasses the two identities in relation with each other.

We are always working within a multi- or cross-cultural context, as no two people have the exact same context. Even in a shared culture, the experience is different for both people. All counselling and therapy practice involves working cross-culturally because every single client and every single counsellor has their own unique culture, identity and lived experience, and being in a therapeutic relationship means a relationship between two unique identities, diversities and cultures. Belonging to a particular culture, ethnicity, race or faith doesn't automatically equip us with the knowledge or understanding of its impact on our client's sense of self, identity, lived experiences and relationships.

When the concept of 'working within diversity' is located within the therapeutic relationship, it becomes a core, embedded and integral part of the therapeutic relationship. 'Working within diversity' is an integral component of a therapeutic relationship that acknowledges both practitioner and client within the relationship, as well as both of their identities and how the relationship is a result of those two identities working together and relating to one another.

'Working with diversity' is the equivalent of taking yourself as the counsellor and placing yourself outside the counselling room and observing the client through the window because it implies you not being in relationship or in the room as a whole person, or your identity in relationship with the client's whole identity. However, 'working within diversity' places both the counsellor and client fully in the counselling room, where both of their identities are proactive within the relationship.

'Working within diversity' places at the very front and centre of the work, the identity of both counsellor and client and then the two whole identities in the relationship that is unfolding in the counselling process. It allows us to be far more conscious of the whole identity of both the counsellor and the client in the relationship and in the room. This enables us to pay attention to how and why the relationship is unfolding and playing out in the way that it is 'in here' because we can understand how identity or identity characteristics are interacting with one another and influencing the relationship. We are then able to offer space 'in here' to fully and truly honour and value the identity, lived experiences and sense of self of the client and how they are creating and building their relationship with us, as their counsellor.

Principle 6: Culturally attuned

Discussions and reflections on 'working within diversity' always remind me why the term 'cultural competency' or 'competencies' in 'working with' culture or race training, as a stand-alone skill, is problematic. Cultural competence indicates an understanding of concepts and knowledge to do with identity and diversity. This is the information, understanding, knowledge and reading around and about the topic of diversity and identity that we do and gain outside the counselling room. It implies a finish line to reach and illustrates and reinforces the power the counsellor holds, via knowledge, competency of knowledge and cognitive or academic understanding of the topic, which only maintains the power-oppression relational dynamic between counsellor and client, with the counsellor maintaining a position of 'expert' or expertise over the client.

Instead, we need to be culturally attuned. To be culturally attuned is to encompass and embody cultural curiosity, cultural humility and cultural empathy. It is for us to be intentionally placed in a position of practising, having and offering all these three qualities, as cultural attunement, to clients.

Cultural humility is to be respectful of people's experience of systemic inequalities and their social locations; it asks us to take up a position of humility and non-judgement to everyone and the diverse lived experiences they have had. Cultural empathy is to take up a position of openness and willingness to see the client fully in their intersectional identities and to empathize with their experiences and be willing to feel and be affected by their lived experiences. Cultural curiosity is to approach our work and clients from a position of curiosity and interest, to allow the work to unfold from a place of 'not knowing' and offer the space for clients to make meaning themselves of their lived experiences.

Culture is infinite and evolving in nature. There is no finish line to reach in learning about and understanding culture. Being culturally attuned is an ongoing process. We need to be comfortable in 'not knowing' and to move into a relational position of being at a start line, to attune, explore, be curious and open to the client's lived experience, their truth and their discovery of understanding themselves.

Through this book, we can start to understand the scale of cultural attunement that is required (in training and practice) to offer an anti-oppressive counselling practice.

Principle 7: Re-establishing external contexts
'Working within diversity' adds diversity back into our work as a key part of the context.

Diversity gets repositioned in the external layers of context: the systemic, structural, political, cultural, historical, societal, community and familial contexts (see Figure 2).

Working 'with' has decontextualized diversity (removing the systemic, structural, political, cultural, historical, societal, community and familial contexts) and instead positions diversity as a label and identity of the client, which makes the client accountable for everything they experience at the oppressed end of the power-oppressive dynamic and their experiences of systemic inequality, because of being 'diverse' or 'different'.

When we remove external contexts, the client becomes 'othered' and then blamed or seen at fault if counselling is not working, if they are seen as not helping themselves, or if they are presenting with limited or minimal autonomy and choice. They may be blamed for being unable to make changes or progress in counselling.

Putting external contexts back in, by 'working within diversity', we can acknowledge and honour that our own and our client's lived experiences are shaped by those external contexts. We can acknowledge that the counsellor is not a blank screen, neutral or normative. We can work with and use our understanding of external contexts and systemic and structural frameworks to understand what is happening 'in here', in our therapeutic relationship, and how we work with and contextualize the client's identity, lived experiences, relationships and worldview.

The 'in here' space of the counselling room doesn't live or belong in a vacuum. The 'out there' rest of the world, history, politics, society and culture are all brought into the counselling room, just as counselling exists within the 'out there' world and is not immune or separate from it. Therefore, it is important to understand the systemic, structural, social, economic, political and historical context of society just as much as the systemic, structural, social, economic, philosophical and historical context of the counselling professional and their practice.

Counselling in its nature is political, because we acknowledge our client's lived experiences 'out there', from which their emotional stresses spring and impact them and which are all brought into the 'in here' counselling space. Counselling is political by its very nature of acknowledging that a client's lived experiences 'out there' are due to the political, social, cultural, historical or systemic inequalities and context within which clients navigate their lives. The 'out there' experience becomes an internalized worldview – an internal view of who they are in the world, how they are seen and treated by the world and how they see themselves.

By re-establishing external contexts and recognizing that all the external contexts are brought into the 'in here' context, we can work with and understand how they impact on the therapeutic process, experience and therapeutic relationship. The 'out there' contexts and internalized 'out there' experience are present and proactive 'in here' and in the process and relationship. We can't ignore them or keep them 'out there'.

Reflective exercises

What are your immediate thoughts, feelings and reflections on learning about the Working within Diversity model and its principles?

....

....

....

....

....

....

In what ways does the Working within Diversity model and its principles support or challenge how you currently approach your therapeutic practice?

....

....

....

....

....

....

What immediately comes to mind when you think about what you need to change, do differently or think about differently in your therapeutic practice?

....

....

....

....

....

....

What questions come to mind from reading this chapter on Working within Diversity?

....

....

....

....

....

....

Part 1: Reflections

Now you have deconstructed 'working with diversity' and been introduced to 'working within diversity', how has this changed your understanding of diversity or diversity training?

....

....

....

....

....

....

Capture any thoughts, reactions and reflections you might have on anything we have covered in Part 1:

....

....

....

....

....

....

Do any questions come up for you about anything covered in Part 1 or do you have a question which you would like to explore in further chapters?

....

....

....

....

....

....

Capture any other thoughts, reactions and reflections you might have in thinking about or applying the Working within Diversity model in your therapeutic practice:

....

....

....

....

....

....

Exploring Diversity and Identity

In Part 2, I will introduce you to and explore an understanding of diversity and identity. Each chapter will present an individual concept, under the topic of diversity and identity, and will cover a definition and summary on each one. This will introduce you to the concepts considered within the Working within Diversity model and its five component parts.

If you would like to read further on any of these topics, there is a recommended reading list at the back of the book.

The concepts introduced in this section include:

- Diversity
- Identity
- Culture
- Honour and shame
- Faith, beliefs and spirituality
- Ethnicity
- Race
- Intersectionality
- Power
- Privilege
- Oppression
- White privilege
- Microaggressions
- Minority or minoritized identities
- Safe spaces and belonging

Reflective exercise

What might be some initial barriers or challenges for you in looking at the topics in this book? What might be your initial reactions to learning about intersectionality, power, privilege and oppression?

....

....

....

....

....

....

....

CHAPTER 3

Diversity and Identity

Diversity

> **Diversity:** the reflection of a medley of identities that makes up the global population, from the intricate combination of identity characteristics within each person and their own sense of self and identity. It acknowledges that each person has their own unique lived experience in the world, their own relationship with the world, its societies, cultures and people, and that no two people have the exact same identity or experience and relationship with the world.

If diversity reflects the spectrum of identity across all people, with everyone holding multiple identities, then we need to understand 'identity' and unpack what that means and looks like, which we will do in the following section.

Reflective exercises

What are your initial thoughts, reactions and reflections on the topic of diversity?

....

....

....

....

....

....

How would you define or describe diversity?

....

....

....

....

....

As a label or category, how do you relate to it? Is it one you adopt and use or one that doesn't fit well with you?

....

....

....

....

....

....

Capture any other thoughts, reactions and reflections you might have on diversity and working with this topic in your therapeutic practice:

....

....

....

....

....

....

Identity

> **Identity:** the combination of different individual internal and external characteristics through which a person identifies themselves and is recognized.

Identity is constructed through different identity characteristics. This has been illustrated in the Identity Wheel tool, with the identity characteristics listed (Figure 3). The Identity Wheel illustrates the different internal (hidden or invisible) characteristics and external (seen or visible) characteristics that make up our identity.

Imagine looking at this Identity Wheel through a telescope or microscope. When we zoom in, we will be able to see the diversity within each of the characteristics. When we zoom out, we will be able to see all the characteristics together and how they relate to one another and the intersectional identities within one person's identity.

Figure 3: Identity Wheel (with identity characteristics) tool

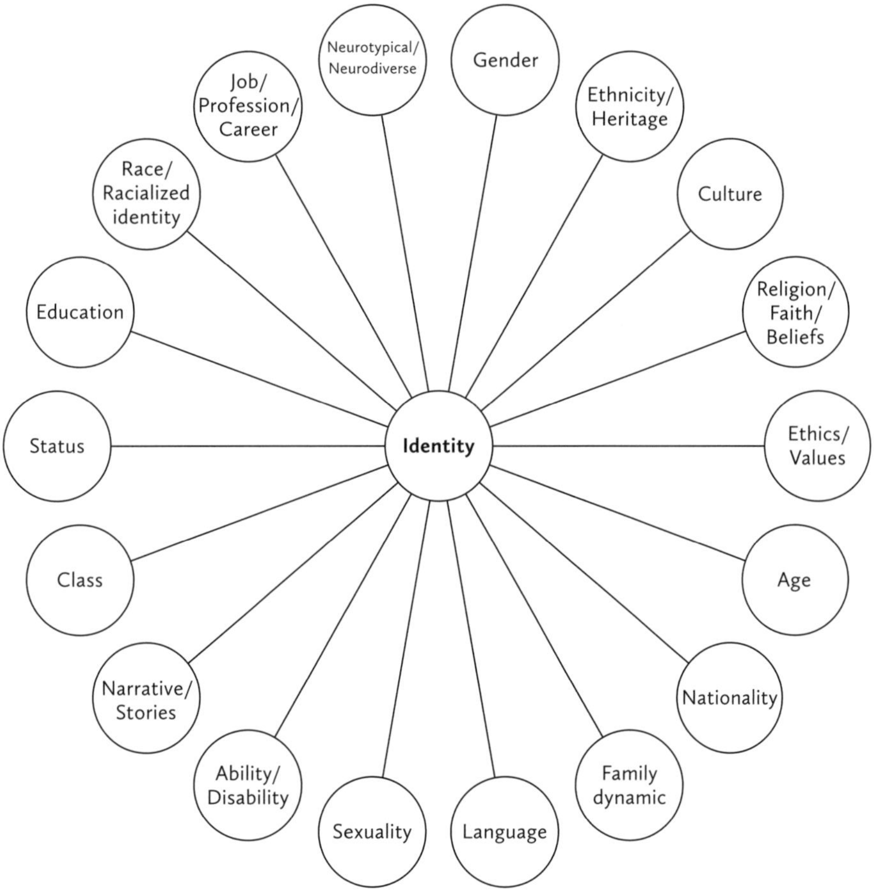

We will be looking in more detail at specific identity characteristics – culture, race, ethnicity and faith/belief/spirituality – in future chapters and exploring how these characteristics piece together. Imagine these identity characteristics as jigsaw puzzle pieces and it's for us to understand what each piece means and how they connect and relate to one another.

We can use the Identity Wheel as a tool to help us identify how we see ourselves and our sense of self. A template of the Identity Wheel tool, which includes the identity characteristics (Figure 3), is also included in the online Appendix.

Activity: Fill in your own Identity Wheel (Figure 4). What would you label for each identity characteristic? How do you self-identify each characteristic? A template of the blank Identity Wheel tool (Figure 4) is also included in the online Appendix.

Figure 4: Identity Wheel tool (template)

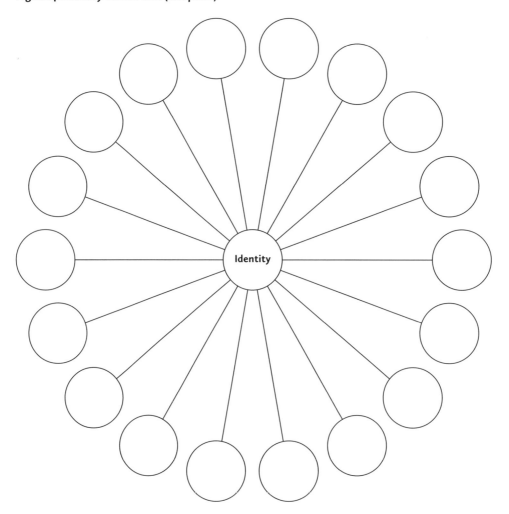

Reflective exercises

What came up for you in doing that exercise? What did you notice or feel? What surprised you? Did you notice if your feelings changed depending on which identity characteristic you were labelling? Which ones were easier or harder to identify?

....

....

....

....

....

....

Are there any other identity characteristics you would like to add to the Identity Wheel?

....

....

....

....

....

....

Which identity characteristics are at the forefront of your identity? Which hold greater weight, significance or importance for you? What makes them significant and important?

....

....

....

....

....

....

Which characteristics do you claim and own? Which ones are in the background or kept hidden?

....

....

....

....

....

....

....

Capture any other thoughts, reactions and reflections you might have on identity and working with this topic in your therapeutic practice:

....

....

....

....

....

....

....

Is this a topic you need to gain more understanding of or read more about? If so, make a note of what questions you might have:

....

....

....

....

....

....

In the next three chapters (Chapters 4–6), we will focus on four of these identity characteristics: culture, faith/belief/spirituality, ethnicity and race. In later chapters (Chapters 7–11) we will look in further depth at the experiences of power, privilege and oppression due to our identity characteristics.

CHAPTER 4

Culture

> **Culture:** a co-created and shared structure of rules and behaviours, values and ethics, ideas and beliefs, habits, practices and traditions, relational and social systems, and language and communication, which is active and evolving and within which a social group, family or community collectively functions.

We all come from specific cultural positions that we tend to inherit from our families and previous generations, as culture is transmitted and handed down through generations, as if we are handed a guidebook on how to understand and make meaning of the world and its cultural contexts being experienced. However, each person will experience their shared culture from their unique and individual perspective, and so culture itself becomes subjective and viewed through that individual's worldview lens.

Our worldview is constructed as a culturally, socially, politically, historically, generationally, systemically, structurally determined lens. How we see the world is shaped through that lens. The lens itself is influenced and constructed by culture, so there is a direct relationship and feedback loop between culture and the individual's worldview and experience of culture. This is because the culture we grow up in and surround ourselves with develops and influences our sense of self and identity. Culture constructs our worldview, experience of the world (which could be labelled as our frame of reference) and how we interact with the world. Therefore, culture is an integral part of our sense of self, relationships and identity. As culture is not a fixed state but active, the changing and evolving beliefs, ideas, values and practices continue to influence the client's experience and worldview, which in return influences that evolving culture (Cameron, 2020; Eleftheriadou, 1994).

Hofstede, Hofstede and Monkov's model of culture (2010) presents a way of understanding culture through a set of dimensions, which reflect the differing values across cultures. Each culture can be located on each of the four dimensions, to identify the dominant cultural values that culture upholds. In identifying the cultural values in any group, this model supports an understanding of what the cultural messages and narratives are and how a culture reflects and expects its group members to behave within its group.

The four dimensions of culture are:

1. Power distance: the extent to which non-dominant groups accept systemic, structural and social inequalities, and how those inequalities are dealt with. In societies with high levels of power distance, inequalities are not challenged. In societies with low levels of power distance, inequalities are challenged and societies strive towards equality of power.
2. Uncertainty avoidance: the extent to which group members feel unsettled by uncertainty and seek to avoid it. In societies with high levels of uncertainty avoidance, behavioural and belief systems are established to tolerate and attempt to control the uncertainty, to make it feel more certain and settled. In societies with low levels of uncertainty avoidance, behavioural and belief systems are either not established or more relaxed, as they are able to tolerate the uncertainty.
3. Masculinity-femininity: the extent to which society prefers and supports either 'masculine' or 'feminine' characteristics, values and beliefs in their culture. 'Masculine' cultures value assertiveness, achievement and success, leading to a society with a high value on competition. At the other end of the dimension, 'feminine' cultures value cooperation and collaboration, leading to a society with a high value on group consensus and community focus. It has been suggested that the 'masculinity-femininity' dimension could also be known as the 'tough-tender' dimension.
4. Individualism-collectivism: the extent to which identity is located and based in a collective social structure or based in the individual. In some (usually Western) cultures, a greater emphasis is placed on the individualistic notion of self as 'I', supporting an individualistic culture. In some (usually non-Western) cultures, a greater emphasis is placed on the collectivist notion of self as 'we', supporting a collectivist culture.

The individualism-collectivism dimension (Figure 5) is an important one to consider as part of understanding identity and identity characteristics, as it not only underpins our experience of culture but also has a direct impact on our identity and sense of self and how we see ourselves. This is one aspect of our identity which is created from our cultural experience and influences whether we see our self as an 'I' or 'we'. Do I call myself an 'I' or 'we', that is, do I come from a collectivist or individualist culture?

Figure 5: Collectivist-individualist culture dimension

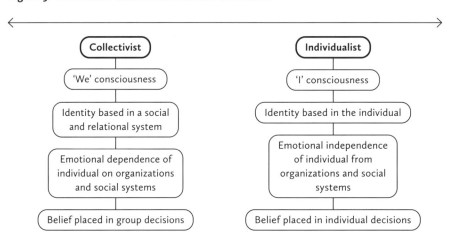

In an individualist culture, the identity of members is centred on the individual 'I', which values autonomy, being self-directed and having individual choice and control. In a collectivist culture, the identity of members is centred on the collective 'we', which values group decisions and being within social and relational systems of dependence, and identity that places power with the group and not individual autonomy. There is a high level of loyalty shown to the family and collective group. As collectivist cultures are highly prevalent in ethnically minoritized cultures, there is often a strong link and overlap between culture and ethnicity. Where ethnically minoritized people are from collectivist cultures, they will most likely have a sense of self as a 'we' (see Figure 6).

Figure 6: Boundary around self as 'we' versus boundary around self as 'I'

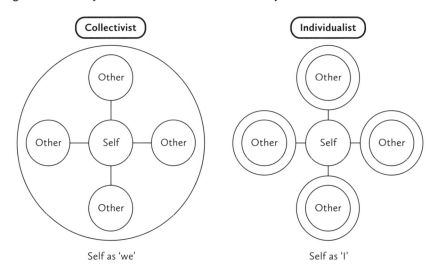

The difference in an identity of 'I' and 'we' can clearly be seen in the boundaries around their sense of self. For the individualist 'I' there are boundaries around their individual sense of self, whereas for the collectivist 'we' there is a lack of boundaries (internally and externally) in their individual sense of self as their sense of self incorporates other people whom they are in relationship with and so they have a collective sense of self and identity (see Figure 6).

Reflective exercises

Can you identify if you are from an individualist or collectivist culture or upbringing? Do you say 'I' or 'we'? And how does it feel to now notice that you self-identify in that way?

....

....

....

....

....

....

....

In what way may you have changed from an individualist to collectivist culture, or from a collectivist to individualist culture? Or have you experienced a merge or holding of both cultures?

....

....

....

....

....

....

....

What beliefs and values have you learned from your culture? Are these beliefs and values you hold yourself now? Which of your cultural beliefs and values do you agree and disagree with?

....

....

....

....

....

....

....

What values, belief or thoughts do you hold about individualist cultures?

....

....

....

....

....

....

....

What values, beliefs or thoughts do you hold about collectivist cultures?

....

....

....

....

....

....

....

Does one culture feel more comfortable to you than the other?

....

....

....

....

....

....

....

Which ancestral events, and cultural values and beliefs, have shaped or influenced your personal identity?

....

....

....

....

....

....

....

Capture any other thoughts, reactions and reflections you might have on culture and working with this topic in your therapeutic practice:

....

....

....

....

....

....

....

Is this a topic you need to gain more understanding of or read more about? If so, make a note of what questions you might have:

....

....

....

....

....

....

Honour

> **Honour:** external status or reputation of an individual, which is upheld through honourable behaviours and actions.

I wanted to give 'honour' and 'shame' a special mention, as they are words often used to act as a barrier to counselling but are very powerful relational and cultural dynamics which influence a person's choice or autonomy, keeping a person stuck or trapped within their cultural, community or familial role, especially if they come from an 'honour culture'.

Honour is being thought about in this context as the external status or reputation of an individual, upheld through honourable behaviours and actions, as an allegiance to their family or community's social rules. These honourable behaviours then reflect the honour (status and reputation) of the entire family. This is not about honour as the internal feeling of self-esteem, self-value or integrity, but an external sign of being honourable and living within an 'honour culture' (Vandello & Cohen, 2003).

Honour derives from relational, cultural and traditionally held values and beliefs, communicated through verbal and non-verbal rules and codes. Every member of the family or group knows what the honourable behaviours, actions and rules are, and what are deemed shameful behaviours and actions. The honourable and shameful behaviours are shared common rules for all members of the group, known as honour codes.

Honour codes are prevalent in collectivist cultures due to the nature of the group's social and relational systems of dependence, which place power with the group and not individual autonomy. This leads to the need and pressure to uphold honour codes by the individual, as it becomes a reflection of the collective family's honour, and therefore a reflection of the whole family.

However, most crucially, the emphasis is often placed on the women within the family, as the carriers of their family honour. The honourable behaviours are visible for public viewing and outwardly directed, so that the wider family and community can see that the women maintain the honour and the honour is carried as a status by the whole family. Family honour is most often determined by the social and sexual behaviour of any or all daughters. It is often aligned to what is expected of and from the daughters in the family and then the daughters fulfilling those expectations. This can include unmarried women – often female young adults – not associating or being seen with non-family male relations without proper supervision, dating or being in a partner (non-married) relationship. Any type of sexual behaviour is a serious breach of family honour. It could also include expectations around education and employment, which can differ between families and communities. For some communities, there could be the expectation to finish school at 16 or 18 years old and get married, which could also include an arranged marriage, through to expectations on others to go to university and get a degree and then get married (which could also include an arranged marriage).

There is no single honour code which is common across all communities but instead honour codes that are common to all members within that community or family. There are serious consequences when honour codes or rules have been breached or broken, including being shunned, ostracized or shut out from the family or community, or more violent consequences such as being physically, psychologically and emotionally abused, and in extreme cases, the threat of or carried out 'honour' killings (Vandello & Cohen, 2003).

Shame

> **Shame:** internal feeling and belief that an individual's own self is all bad, because of having behaved in an exposing, dishonourable manner, with others also viewing them in a negative light.

Shame is the emotional response when an honour code has been breached and the honour held by the family is lost. The distinction between honour and shame is that honour is carried by the whole family, as a collective value and status. At the point the honour is breached, the honour (status and reputation) is lost, and the shame, which is felt by the whole family, gets located and held in the individual who 'lost' the honour through their dishonourable behaviour.

The opposite to honour, which is externally shown and displayed, shame is internally directed and concealed and kept hidden from view by the individual. Shame is a powerful and all-consuming feeling, as the individual feels that they are the mistake, they are bad, rather than thinking they have made a mistake or have done something bad. It becomes about their sense of self and identity, not an external behaviour or a moment of doing something wrong.

Shame then becomes two-fold. First, it results in the shameful external social consequence of their loss of honour, status, reputation and social standing, with others looking on that individual in a negative, contemptable manner (known as external shame). Second, it results in the internal emotional consequence of the individual feeling all bad about themselves, that they are a bad person (known as internal shame). This combination of both external shame (being seen by others negatively) and internal shame (seeing self as all bad) is known as the 'exposed self'. This can leave the individual finding that their external world (other people) and internal world (own sense of self) have turned against them and they are living in an (external and internal) hostile and punitive world (Gilbert & Procter, 2006).

The fear of carrying that shame, shame-based punishment or coming to more serious harm (shame-based harm) is the threat through which the individual is subtly pressurized to uphold the family honour.

Reflective exercises

What are your immediate thoughts, reactions and feelings to thinking about honour and shame? How might you think about and understand honour codes and the feeling of shame?

....

....

....

....

....

....

....

....

Can you identify any behaviours, actions or roles which are a display of honour or honour codes for a family, community or culture?

....

....

....

....

....

....

....

What are your immediate thoughts, reactions and feelings to shame-based harm, punishment or violence and working with it in your therapeutic practice?

....

....

....

....

....

....

....

Is this a topic you need to gain more understanding of or read more about? If so, make a note of what questions you might have:

....

....

....

....

....

....

CHAPTER 5

Faith, Beliefs and Spirituality

Faith: a defined or strong belief in a religion or belief system.

Religion: a recognized belief system of faith, which includes the belief in a higher power, God or Gods, and worship through prayer, religious practices or rituals.

Belief system: a set of principles, values and beliefs which form a moral and ethical code and worldview.

Spirituality: a belief beyond the self and a connection between the self and others, the world and other realms, which can be reflected through spiritual practices.

Reflective exercises

What comes to mind when you think of the below words and what does each word mean to you?

Faith:

....

....

....

....

....

....

Religion:

....

....

....

....

....

....

Belief system:

....

....

....

....

....

....

Spirituality:

....

....

....

....

....

....

What other words or terms might you also use instead of 'faith'?

....

....

....

....

....

....

Religion, faith, belief and spiritual practice can support the construction of people's worldviews, giving meaning to their lives through practices, rituals and concepts about the purpose of their life and how to live a life aligned with an ethical and moral compass.

Religion, faith, belief and spiritual practice can offer meaning about life and are often leant on to help support people when they are facing difficulties, reinforcing resilience and strength to get through and bear distressing experiences. Religion, faith, belief and spiritual practice also offer a source of understanding, hope and healing, in particular offering guidance when things go wrong or are difficult and challenging.

Like every other identity characteristic, it is crucial to understand the importance of a person's faith, belief or spirituality not only in their life but also in the construction of their sense of self and identity.

Let's take some time to think about what faith, religion, belief or spirituality means to you and your identity.

Reflective exercises

Spirituality guided visualization exercise
I will walk you through a series of prompts to help you visualize what spirituality means for you.

Open your hands and imagine you are holding spirituality in the palm of your hands like an object.

- What is the shape and size of it?
- What is its weight?
- What is its colour?
- Does it make a sound or is it silent? If a sound, what sound?
- Does it have a scent, smell or fragrance?
- What are you feeling as you hold the object?
- What do you want to do with the object?

Now place the object somewhere safe for you. Capture any thoughts or feelings you are left with:

....

....

....

....

....

....

....

Reflect on your answers. What does this reveal about your relationship with spirituality?

....

....

....

....

....

....

....

Has anything surprised you about your answers?

....

....

....

....

....

....

....

Can you identify your faith, religious, belief system or spirituality upbringing? In what way may that have changed for you throughout your life?

....

....

....

....

....

....

....

Can you identify your current faith, religious, belief system or spirituality? Do you have a faith, belief system or spirituality that is important to you?

....

....

....

....

....

....

What is your current relationship and experience with religion, a belief system or a spiritual practice? What is the relationship between your faith, belief system or spirituality and your identity as a whole? Does it hold significant value in your identity, or a lesser value?

....

....

....

....

....

....

What beliefs and values do you hold from your faith, belief system or spirituality? Which of your faith or spiritual beliefs and values do you find easier or more challenging to practise?

....

....

....

....

....

....

....

What values, beliefs or thoughts do you hold about other faiths, belief systems or spiritual practices?

....

....

....

....

....

....

Does one faith, belief system or spirituality (that you don't belong to or identify with) feel more comfortable for you to be in relationship (or emotional contact) with than another?

....

....

....

....

....

....

Capture any other thoughts, reactions and reflections you might have on faith, beliefs and spirituality and working with this topic in your therapeutic practice:

....

....

....

....

....

....

Is this a topic you need to gain more understanding of or read more about? If so, make a note of what questions you might have:

....

....

....

....

....

....

CHAPTER 6

Ethnicity and Race

Ethnicity

> **Ethnicity:** a group of people who share a collective cultural, historical, geographical heritage passed generationally through families and communities.

The shared and collective nature of the group supports a psychological and relational bond and an emotional need to feel a sense of belonging and connectedness with one another and feel part of a group. This relational and shared collective culture distinguishes ethnicity from race and racialized identities, in which race is based on a social construct of defining people by reductive external observable factors such as skin colour, without acknowledging or recognizing the relational and group dynamics contained within a group's shared culture, history or heritage.

As ethnicity is so closely linked and expressed through the culture of an ethnically identified group or heritage, learning about culture will help support your understanding of the relational and collective structures and dynamics of any group. See Chapter 4 for further information about culture.

Ethnicity is one characteristic of a person's identity, as well as being one of the spectrums of oppression. A person's ethnicity influences how they are related to in society. By learning about intersectionality and systems of oppression we can support our understanding of how and why different ethnically identified groups are viewed, treated and related to, within the social structure, by one another. See Chapter 7 for further information about ethnicity as part of intersectional identity and as a system of oppression. See Chapter 9 for further information about the difference between ethnicity viewed as a 'minority' and minoritized identity.

Reflective exercises

What might be the impact of ethnicity on a person's lived experience?

....

....

....

....

....

....

....

Based on your own experiences, how do you define your own ethnicity?

....

....

....

....

....

....

Based on your own experiences, how do others define your ethnicity, especially on first meeting you? What differences do you notice between how you self-identify and how others identify you?

....

....

....

....

....

....

How do you or others define your ethnicity, and in what way may that have changed for you throughout your life?

....

....

....

....

....

....

What is your current relationship and experience with your ethnicity? What is the relationship between your ethnicity and your identity as a whole? Does it hold significant value in your identity or a lesser value?

....

....

....

....

....

....

....

What aspects (cultural, historical, geographical or generational) within your ethnicity are significant or important to you? Which aspects hold less value or importance?

....

....

....

....

....

....

....

What beliefs and values do you hold about your ethnicity? Are any beliefs and values more challenging to deal with?

....

....

....

....

....

....

What beliefs and values do others hold about your ethnicity? Are any beliefs and values more challenging to deal with? Might they appear as stereotypes and affect how you are treated because of those stereotypes?

....

....

....

....

....

....

What values, beliefs, thoughts or stereotypes do you hold about other ethnicities? Where did these come from? Are they cultural-, societal- or community-held beliefs or stereotypes?

....

....

....

....

....

....

....

Does one ethnicity (that you don't belong to or identify with) feel more comfortable for you to be in relationship (or emotional contact) with than another?

....

....

....

....

....

....

Capture any other thoughts, reactions and reflections you might have on ethnicity and working with this topic in your therapeutic practice:

....

....

....

....

....

....

Is this a topic you need to gain more understanding of or read more about? If so, make a note of what questions you might have:

....

....

....

....

....

....

....

Race

> **Race:** a social construct of defining people by reductive external observable factors such as skin colour, without acknowledging or recognizing a group's shared culture, history, ethnicity or heritage, or any other identity characteristic.

Race as a social construct is different from the concept of racialized identity and it is important to understand the distinction between the two. Race is the racial category or label assigned to the person. Racialized identity acknowledges the relationship between the dominant group assigning the race label to the non-dominant group and acknowledges this action as a form of oppression.

To have a race identity (a label assigned to you) is different to having a racialized identity (the oppressive relationship and process of a label being assigned to you by the dominant group). For example, I don't say my race (identity label) is Brown but instead I say my racialized identity (how I am being racially identified by the dominant group) is Brown.

Alongside the distinction between race and racialized identity, it is also important to understand the distinction between race and ethnicity. Not only are race and ethnicity two distinct identity characteristics in themselves but each has their own historical and socio-political context and experiences. There is also a difference in how a person may relate to and resonate with each identity characteristic in their internal and external sense of self and identity, as well as how that person is related to and socially located and how each of their identity characteristics positions and influences their intersectional identity and lived experiences (Lago, 1996).

Race, as a social construct, is a system of oppression, resulting in the power-oppression relational dynamic between the dominant, white racialized identity and the non-dominant Black and Brown racialized identity. We can't think about race without thinking about its underlying power differential and the resulting systemic and structural inequalities functioning to uphold the dominant group and their position of power and privilege (Wheeler, 2006).

Bringing awareness of race, as a system of oppression, as an exercise of power over another social group and as a power differential and relational dynamic, we can start to identify and understand how the systems we operate in offer advantages, benefits and privileges to the group that takes up the dominant position, by oppressing, marginalizing and minoritizing another group into a non-dominant position.

Slavery and colonialism are two systems of oppression. These are and were enacted by white supremacy (the superior dominant racial identity group) over identity groups which were racialized, ethnically minoritized and positioned as inferior, and given labels of inferiority by the dominant group, which did and does not self-identify as a racial, minority or inferior identity group. (See Chapter 9 for further discussion on the use of 'minority or minoritized identity' language.)

Race, as a system of oppression, signals to us the power differential between white and Black and Brown racialized identity groups and that the very structure of society is built on a racialized power differential between oppressor and oppressed identity groups. This can be a challenge to members of the white racialized identity group because it is the spotlight on an unequal system of power-oppression, in which they sit at the power, dominant, superior position, benefitting from the advantages and privileges of belonging to the dominant identity group (Lago, 1996; Eddo-Lodge, 2017) (see Chapter 10 for further discussion on 'white privilege').

Reflective exercises

What might be the impact of race on a person's lived experience?

....

....

....

....

....

....

....

How did you learn about race? Was it through lived experience and your upbringing? Or was it through being taught it in a teaching experience and educational setting?

....

....

....

....

....

....

How do you self-identify with race or perhaps you do not self-identify with race?

....

....

....

....

....

....

....

How old were you when you noticed your race or how you were being racialized? Is there a particular story or narrative to that experience? How did you feel?

....

....

....

....

....

....

....

Based on your own experiences, how do you get racialized by others? What differences do you notice between how you self-identify and how others racialize you?

....

....

....

....

....

....

....

How do you or others define your race? In what way may that have changed for you throughout your life?

....

....

....

....

....

....

....

What is your current relationship and experience with your racialized identity or how others racialize you? What is the relationship between your race and your identity as a whole? Does it hold significant value in your identity or not?

....

....

....

....

....

....

What beliefs and values do you hold about your race or racialized identity? Are any beliefs and values more challenging to deal with?

....

....

....

....

....

....

....

Capture any other thoughts, reactions and reflections you might have on race and working with this topic in your therapeutic practice:

....

....

....

....

....

....

Racism

Racism: a form of oppression occurring at the point where power and prejudice meet. The dominant racialized identity group utilizes their power, based on prejudice towards the non-dominant racialized identity group, to harm, harass, invalidate, marginalize, minimize, dismiss, exclude and silence and to relate to and position them as powerless, while maintaining the systems and structures that offer advantages, benefits and privileges to their own dominant group.

Racism is an oppressive relational dynamic from oppressor to the oppressed. Racism is not just about difference; it also involves the full spectrum of power differences and imbalances, from one end of supremacy, privilege and structural/societal advantages through to trauma, oppression, inequalities, marginalization and being minoritized at the other end.

Race and oppression, and their existence, reinforcement and continuing impact through privilege, supremacy, dominance, and systemic and structural advantages, reinforce this racial hierarchy, with white supremacy at the top. This is also to acknowledge both the current and historical trauma of racialized communities, particularly in relation to the 'British Empire', colonialism and slavery.

There are four dimensions of racism (Thomas, 2022; Eddo-Lodge, 2017):

1. Structural racism: as the result of the collective biases and prejudices in a group, built into the infrastructure and social and cultural fabric, embedded across multiple organizations and institutions within their very systems and structures.

2. Institutional racism: as the result of the collective biases and prejudices in a group, built into an organization or institution's policies, mechanisms, standards and internal political, social and cultural practices.

3. Interpersonal racism: as the result of an individual's biases and prejudices, acted out through their behaviours, actions and microaggressions towards another person (their target).

4. Individual or internalized racism: a form of internalized oppression. Negative beliefs and messages, once directed at an individual externally from the oppressor, now get internalized and the oppressed self-direct those messages and beliefs towards themselves, reinforcing the original oppressor's racism towards them.

Reflective exercises

What beliefs and values or prejudices do others hold about your race? Are any beliefs and values more challenging to deal with? How have you experienced racism towards yourself?

....

....

....

....

....

....

What might be the impact, barriers or challenges you have experienced because of racism?

....

....

....

....

....

....

What values, beliefs, thoughts, stereotypes or prejudices do you hold about other racialized groups? Where did these come from? Are they cultural-, societal-, community-held beliefs or stereotypes?

....

....

....

....

....

Does one racialized group (that you don't belong to or identify with) feel more comfortable for you to be in relationship (or emotional contact) with than another?

....

....

....

....

....

....

Colour-blindness

Colour-blindness: to deny seeing colour as a racial identifier and being blind to and denying that different racialized identities and racial inequalities exist.

Colour-blindness removes the system of oppression as if it doesn't exist, on the insistence that race doesn't impact on a person's lived experience, social location and access to resources and opportunities. This eliminates the recognition of the presence of systemic inequality and therefore the presence of systems of oppression that benefit and privilege the dominant identity groups and oppress the non-dominant identity groups. Colour-blindness eliminates the accountability, responsibility ʃand consequences of oppression from dominant groups towards non-dominant groups (Eddo-Lodge, 2017; Cameron, 2020; D'Ardenne & Mahtani, 1989).

Colour-blindness is not the same as being anti-racist, where you are proactively acknowledging race and racism and working to flatten the power of that bias and prejudice.

Being an 'anti-racist' is not being 'colour-blind' or saying 'I don't see colour'. It is when you're acknowledging a person's lived experiences and trauma of being oppressed, minimized, dismissed, discounted and humiliated because of their ethnicity.

Reflective exercises

What has been your experience of colour-blindness? How has colour-blindness shown up in your work, social or community spaces and relationships?

....

....

....

....

....

....

Have you been treated with colour-blindness? What did that experience feel like? What did you notice about what was happening to your identity? Were you feeling missed, dismissed or made invisible?

....

....

....

....

....

....

Capture any other thoughts, reactions and reflections you might have on col-our-blindness and working with this topic in your therapeutic practice:

....

....

....

....

....

....

Is this a topic you need to gain more understanding of or read more about? If so, make a note of what questions you might have:

....

....

....

....

....

....

The interconnectedness between culture, faith, ethnicity and race

Considering the four identity characteristics of culture, faith, ethnicity and race, we can start to recognize the importance that all of them play within a person's identity and intersectionality and perhaps how the four characteristics themselves overlap, interact with and influence one another.

For example, religion can provide the principles, values and beliefs in life for an individual, while culture and ethnicity can play a crucial role in the expression or practice of their religion or faith.

It is important to know the tenets of cultural worldviews as well as our religious and ethnic worldviews and lived experiences all contained within our identity and intersectional identities. While it is important to understand the religious, cultural and ethnic components of a person's identity, we also need to be sensitive to the uniqueness of an individual, their intersectional identities and their lived experiences.

Reflective exercise

Capture any other thoughts, reactions and reflections you might have on culture, faith, ethnicity or race and working with these topics in your therapeutic practice:

....

....

....

....

....

....

CHAPTER 7

Intersectionality and Identity

> **Intersectionality:** the point at which a person's multiple privileged, oppressed and marginalized identity characteristics intersect.

Kimberlé Crenshaw (1989) conceptualized the term intersectionality, which is a framework for understanding how people are located on a power-oppression spectrum and identifies how much power and privilege they hold or the degree of oppression they experience, based on their identity characteristics, such as race, class, gender and ethnicity, and all other identity characteristics as listed on the Identity Wheel (see Figure 3).

Intersectionality offers a structure to identify how and where a person's privileged and oppressed identity characteristics intersect on the power-oppression spectrum (also known as the spectrum of oppression). This helps to locate and understand the person's social position and lived experience within systemic and structural frameworks of inequality. It allows for all the multiple identity characteristics (on the Identity Wheel) to be acknowledged within one person and how the multiple privileged and oppressed identities co-exist as well as reinforce one another and their overall sense of self (Eddo-Lodge, 2017; Thomas, 2022).

Intersectionality helps us to understand how and why people experience both privileges, due to their advantaged identities, and inequalities, through oppressive barriers, marginalization and minoritization, due to their disadvantaged identity characteristics. This is weighted especially towards visible identity characteristics such as race, ethnicity, gender, visible ability, visible faith and age.

Intersectionality can also be referred to as 'intersectional identities'. Each person has an intersectionality (or intersectional identity). It is imperative to remember that intersectionality (intersectional identities) recognizes and acknowledges both a person's privileged (advantaged) identities and their oppressed (disadvantaged) identities, rather than only highlighting their oppressed identities and avoiding, denying or minimizing their privileged (advantaged) identities (Eddo-Lodge, 2017; Winer, 2021; Thomas, 2022).

If intersectionality is not taught during our counselling or psychotherapy training then we will never fully understand the power dynamics and relationships at play in our society, in our profession, in our clinical practice, in our lived experiences and in our clients' lived experiences. We could even say that this is privilege in action. If it is not being talked about itself then power, embedded within the professional system and structures, is being exerted across the teaching curriculum to oppress the discussion and understanding of it. Opportunities within therapeutic practice to develop an understanding of how intersectionality is being repeated in the 'in here' space and relationship and to work with it consciously with our clients are also being oppressed.

Social identity and systems of oppression

To understand intersectionality is to also understand the relationship between our identity, how we experience the world and the quality of that relationship. Based on our identity characteristics we are socially located within societal demographics and categories. Depending on which demographics and categories we are assigned to, we are treated in a particular way regarding the degree of power, privilege and status which gets attributed to our advantaged identity characteristics or the level of oppression and prejudice we experience because of our disadvantaged identity characteristics.

When we, in our full identity and cultural selves, go out into the world, we are socially located on a 'global identity map' – we are categorized and identified based on our identity and identity characteristics. Our identity in relationship with the world/society and being socially located creates our lived experience (see Figure 7).

Figure 7: Social location on the 'global identity map'

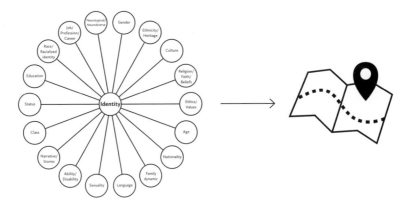

Our lived experience (our relationships, our emotional experiences, our social and cultural experiences, the messages we are given because of our identity, how we are treated because of our identity, the privileges and oppressions we experience) becomes our internal world and provides internalized messages about who we are and where we belong in society (dominant high social status or non-dominant low social status).

Our external visible identity and internal identity and sense of self are in a constant feedback loop. Our external identity and social location determine how we are related to in the world, which gets internalized and becomes part of our internal sense of self and identity. Our internal sense of self and identity then impacts on how we feel about our external identity, which is the visible identity that then goes out into the world and gets socially located. Our lived experience is constantly being taken in and internalized and integrated into our internal sense of self, which then becomes the hidden part of our external identity which goes back out into the world (see Figure 8).

Negative external world experiences damage our internal sense of self, leading to possible internalized feelings of an unsafe, anxious and threatening view of the world. Positive external world experiences support a positive internal sense of self, with feelings of being safe, welcomed, belonging to and in relationship with the world.

Figure 8: Relationship between cultural identity and social location

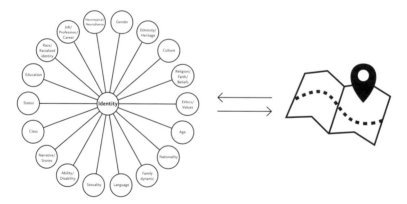

Being socially located on the 'global identity map' means getting located on systems of oppression based on your identity. A system (or spectrum) of oppression has at one end dominant high social status identity groups (privileged and advantaged identities) and at the other end non-dominant low social status identity groups (oppressed and disadvantaged identities). The degree of power, value and status you are ascribed is based on your identity and combination of identity characteristics.

The system of oppression is a hierarchy and power relational dynamic between dominant (advantaged) and non-dominant (disadvantaged) identity groups.

If we belong to a dominant high social status identity group (and get located at the top end of the spectrum), we occupy the powerful, dominant and advantaged position relationally to the non-dominant group. We receive an abundance of privileges and advantages in society; we identify as the 'normative' identity group within that society and hold a high-power value and status of supremacy.

If we belong to a non-dominant low social status identity group (and get located at the bottom end of the spectrum), we are oppressed into the low-power, marginalized and disadvantaged position relationally, on the receiving end of disadvantages, biases, prejudices, invalidation, barriers to access resources and opportunities, and marginalization, and identified as 'different' from the 'normative' group and labelled as the 'other' (the process of othering). This oppression is upheld by the dominant high social status group through systemic and structural inequalities embedded in society. This ultimately leads to the societal disparity and inequalities we see between dominant and non-dominant communities (see Figure 9).

Figure 9: Spectrum of oppression (with status characteristics)

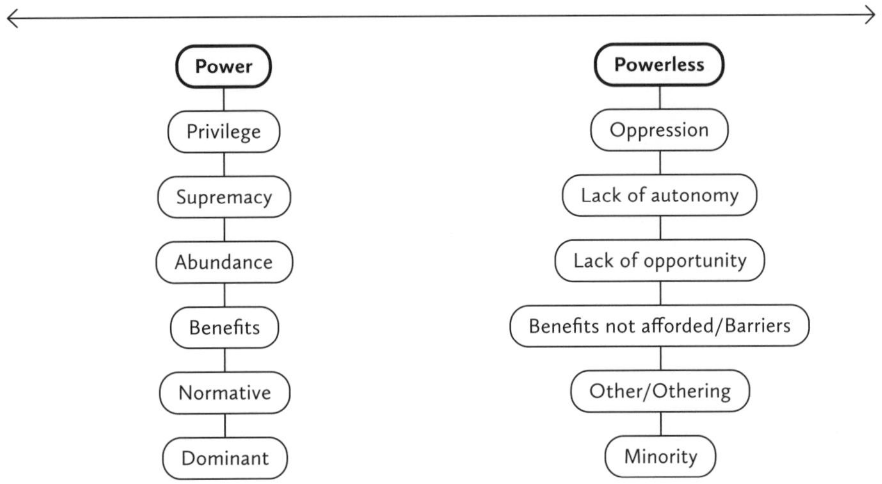

Power	Powerless
Privilege	Oppression
Supremacy	Lack of autonomy
Abundance	Lack of opportunity
Benefits	Benefits not afforded/Barriers
Normative	Other/Othering
Dominant	Minority

Reflective exercise

Regarding identity and identity characteristics, what systems of oppression do you think exist?

....

....

....

....

....

....

For every identity characteristic we have, there is a corresponding system of oppression (see Figure 10). For example, there is a system of oppression for ethnicity, gender, racialized identity, faith, nationality, ability-disability, neurotypical-neurodivergent and for all other identity characteristics. We will be looking at the racialized identity system of oppression in more detail in Chapters 9 and 10.

Figure 10: Examples of spectrums of oppressions

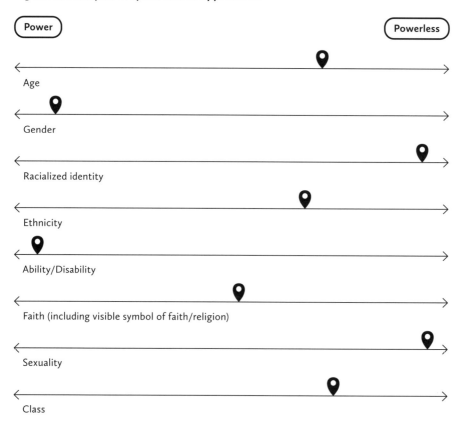

For each system of oppression, you can plot where you land at either the dominant or non-dominant end of the spectrum, depending on your individual identity for that identity characteristic (see Figure 10).

Activity: Where are you on the different systems of oppression? Plot where you land on each spectrum. Please note that a selection of identity characteristics were chosen for the purpose of this exercise, but this does not imply that some identity characteristics are prioritized above or are any more important than others not listed (see Figure 11).

Figure 11: Spectrums of oppressions tool

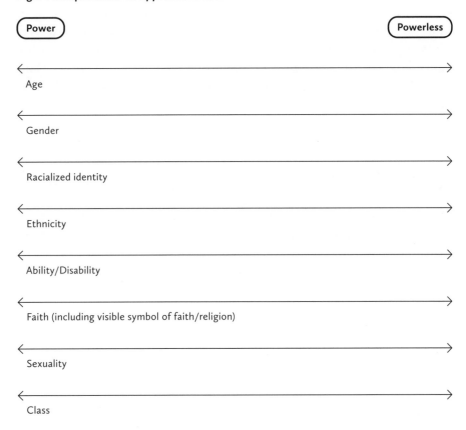

The place where each system of oppression meets, identifies the level of power or oppression you experience because of your identity. This is your intersectionality (or intersectional identity).

As an example for myself I would say that my intersectionality (intersectional identity) is as a hijab-wearing, visibly Muslim, ethnically minoritized Brown, of

East-African Asian heritage, English-speaking, higher-degree educated, self-employed woman.

Deconstructed, my intersectionality (intersectional identity) is a faith identity, ethnically minoritized identity, ethnic heritage identity, first language, education level, employment status and gender identity. You could choose to include additional spectrums of oppression in your description of your intersectionality. Your intersectionality will reflect what privileged (advantaged) and oppressed (disadvantaged) identities you hold. Therefore, everyone has an intersectionality (intersectional identity).

When the development of our sense of self is in direct relationship with our lived experiences in the world, which is based on our intersectionality (intersectional identity), this is where we can start to understand how struggles, challenges or mental health distress (due to our lived experiences, social location and disadvantaged intersectional identity) become located in the individual person. The person becomes held responsible for their distress or trauma rather than it being held within the external social and cultural context of systemic inequality and oppression that they may be experiencing.

Reflective exercises

Based on where you land on the spectrums of oppression, how would you describe your intersectionality (intersectional identity), which includes both your advantaged and disadvantaged identities?

....

....

....

....

....

....

....

....

....

In thinking about your identity, how does it influence how you are treated and related to by society? Which characteristics do you feel have the most impact or stand out the most to others and how others view or perceive you? These may not be the same characteristics as the ones which hold greater weight in your own sense of self and identity.

....

....

....

....

....

....

Capture any other thoughts, reactions, reflections or questions you might have on intersectionality and working with this topic in your therapeutic practice:

....

....

....

....

....

....

Is this a topic you need to gain more understanding of or read more about? If so, make a note of what questions you might have:

....

....

....

....

....

....

CHAPTER 8

Power and Privilege

Power

> **Power:** the ability to access and influence others, to act with autonomy and exercise control, to access resources, spaces and services.

Reflective exercises

What comes to mind when you think of the word 'power'?

....

....

....

....

....

Where or how do you think power shows up?

....

....

....

....

....

Individuals hold power but power is also placed within systems and structures such as money, institutions, laws and history. Power holds influence over others and the quality and type of relationships and experiences people have.

Identity characteristics play a major role in determining social status and access to power, socially locating you on the spectrums of oppression-power. (See Chapter 7 for a more in-depth explanation of systems of oppression.)

Our different identity characteristics mean that we land further up or down the spectrum of oppression according to their value of either being a dominant high value or non-dominant low value.

Our ethnicity, gender, age, ability/disability and racialized identity hold greater weight to how far up or down that spectrum we land because they can be visible characteristics immediately seen, judged and assumed about a person's identity. Where we land on each system of oppression becomes the 'norm' for each of us. Even if you are at the privilege end, and it becomes your norm by default, it still makes it a privilege. A 'norm' doesn't remove either privilege or oppression.

Reflective exercise

Identity characteristics all have their respective system of oppression but what other aspects of our identity hold power? And what might be the result of that power?

....

....

....

....

....

....

We recognize that different aspects of our identity can increase or decrease our power in relation to other people, depending on where we land on systems of oppression. The Scales of Power in Identity Characteristics (Figure 12) identifies some of the identity factors which can increase and decrease our power. Please note that this diagram does not list every dominant and minoritized identity characteristic.

Figure 12: Scales of Power in Identity Characteristics

Increases power ↑

Being:
White racialized
English speaking
Male
Aged between 25 and 45
Middle class or elite
Heterosexual
Non-disabled
Educated
Employed
Attractive

Being:
Ethnically minoritized
Racially minoritized
Non-English speaking
English speaking with a strong regional accent
Female/Non-binary
Young/Old
Working class
LGBTQ+
Disabled
Uneducated
Unemployed

Decreases power ↓

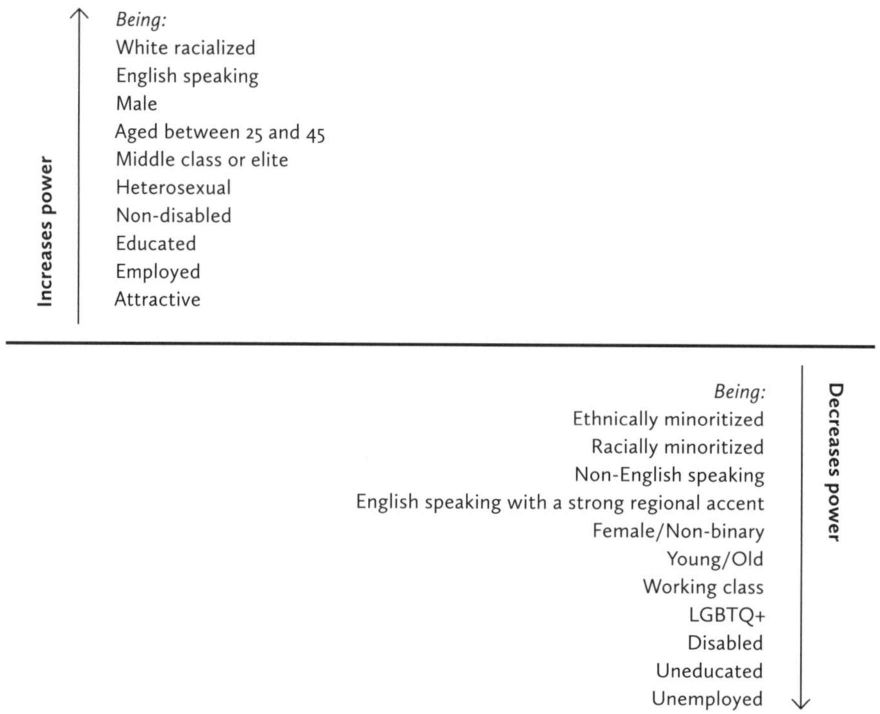

Figure 13: Scales of Power in Identity Characteristics tool (template)

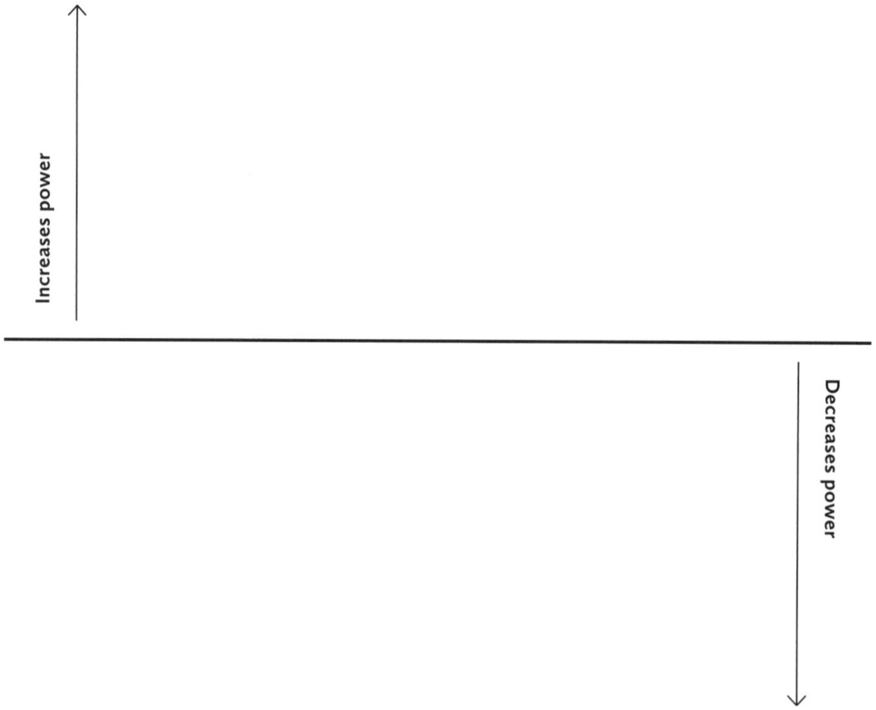

Increases power ↑

Decreases power ↓

Activity: Are there any factors in your lived experience or from your identity characteristics that have had the effect of increasing or decreasing your power? Using your Identity Wheel and intersectional identity description to help you identify the different factors which may increase or decrease your power, complete the Scales of Power in Identity Characteristics (Figure 13) for yourself. A template of the Scales of Power in Identity Characteristics tool is also included in the online Appendix.

Reflective exercises

What are your thoughts, reactions and reflections in filling in these scales? What has come up for you? Were you surprised by what you listed in either scale? How were you surprised?

....

....

....

....

....

....

....

Did any characteristics or aspects of identity appear that you were not expecting? Did more characteristics appear in the scales which increased or decreased your power than you anticipated?

....

....

....

....

....

....

....

By identifying characteristics that increase and decrease your power, how does that show up in how others relate to you, treat you, perceive you or how you are socially located?

....

....

....

....

....

....

Do you have any thoughts on what this might mean for your therapeutic practice and therapeutic relationships at this stage?

....

....

....

....

....

....

The Power Threat Meaning Framework (Johnstone & Boyle, 2018) supports our understanding of how power operates in and impacts our lives. Figure 14 illustrates the four key questions to help us make meaning of our relationship with power. What this framework fundamentally offers is a shift from blame and responsibility on the individual causing their own distress or mental health challenges (which would position it as asking the individual 'what is wrong' with them individually), to a focus on the external context of systemic, structural and social frameworks within which the individual operates and exists. It is therefore the impact from and responsibility of these external contexts on the individual's lived experiences and any distress, trauma and pain they have experienced.

We will be looking at the impact of power held in our identity on therapy and therapeutic relationships in Part 3.

Figure 14: Questions from the Power Threat Meaning Framework (image adapted from Johnstone & Boyle, 2018)

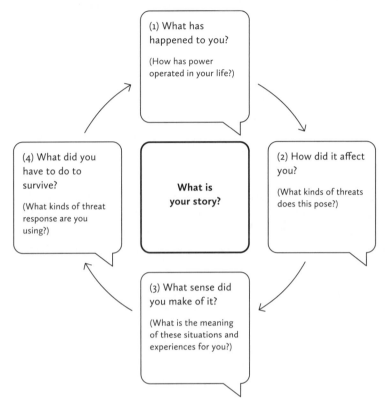

(1) What has happened to you?

(How has power operated in your life?)

What is your story?

(2) How did it affect you?

(What kinds of threats does this pose?)

(3) What sense did you make of it?

(What is the meaning of these situations and experiences for you?)

(4) What did you have to do to survive?

(What kinds of threat response are you using?)

Privilege

> **Privilege:** unearned, automatic benefits and advantages given to members of the dominant high social status majority identity group.

Privilege includes both the presence of an unearned advantage or benefit as well as the absence of a disadvantage or barrier. They are not mutually exclusive. They can exist simultaneously. These can be personal, societal and institutional privileges, such as opportunities, choices, entitlements, responsibilities and positive assumptions, projections and expectations about that person. The person is seen in a positive light and is of high value. Even if these advantages are considered basic human values or rights, when they are only offered to the dominant majority group, and not to the minoritized group, they automatically become privileges.

Being a member of the dominant majority group means that the social system is created for you, works in your favour and automatically gives you unearned benefits (privileges) because of your membership. For those belonging to the minoritized group, the system is not created with them in mind.

The difficulty of spotting privileges for those belonging to the dominant group who are advantaged by privileges is that the privileges are often invisible or unseen by them, because their lived experience is such that the system set up for them becomes their 'norm' and so advantage/privilege is seen as a given, expectation or 'usual' to them. It is a normative position to have in that system and so it isn't seen as a privilege or advantage. Instead, it becomes the 'status quo' of how they experience the world, how they are treated, what they have access to and how there are no barriers to accessing what they want. They also have no understanding that these advantages, privileges and lack of barriers are not the same for everyone and only exist for their dominant group.

Privileges are those benefits that people don't earn but get just because of who they are or are perceived to be. For example, if you work hard to build up your wealth, you receive the earned benefit of getting to buy things. But if you are perceived to be wealthy, you receive the unearned benefit (privilege) of being treated well by society. Systematic targeting and marginalization mean it doesn't happen randomly or by chance, but is doled out according to a part of a fixed system – one that does damage to other people. Also, because people with privilege get more, other people get less just because of who they are.

Power offers privilege to those occupying the privileged position. Privilege highlights that systemic and institutional discrimination still exists. Being aware of privilege increases our awareness of systemic inequalities and the power relational dynamics. It increases our understanding of systems that produce, create and sustain the privileges and in which privilege is set within an oppressive practice and structure to support the advantages of the dominant majority group by oppressing the minoritized group (i.e. giving privilege to one group but not another).

Reflective exercises

What do you understand by the term 'privilege'? What examples of privilege can you think of?

....

....

....

....

....

Which of your identity characteristics are privileged (i.e. an identity that places you at the power end of the spectrum of oppression)?

....

....

....

....

....

In what ways are these identities privileged? What advantages does it give you? Where or how do you think privilege shows up for you? (Remember that the advantage or privilege may be the lack of a barrier rather than the presence of an additional benefit.)

....

....

....

....

....

Is this a topic you need to gain more understanding of or read more about? If so, make a note of what questions you might have. In considering privilege, note down any thoughts of what this might mean for your therapeutic practice and therapeutic relationships:

....

....

....

....

....

CHAPTER 9

Oppression

> **Oppression:** the systematic targeting of a non-dominant low social status group by a dominant high social status group through their power and prejudice. The aim is to marginalize, discriminate and disempower the non-dominant group, so that the dominant group can retain and maintain their systemic and structural power, authority and privilege.

Please see Chapter 1 for how current therapeutic practice on 'working with diversity' is deconstructed and understood as oppressive and what anti-oppressive practice would look like in its place.

Oppression occurs at the point where power and prejudice meet. The dominant group utilize their power, based on prejudice towards the non-dominant group, to harm, harass, invalidate, marginalize, minimize, dismiss, exclude and silence, and to remove and make them believe they have no power, while maintaining the advantages, benefits and privileges afforded to the dominant group (Chinook Fund, 2015; Proctor, 2017).

There are intentional acts of oppression and unintentional acts of oppression. Oppression happens even if people with the privileged identity or trait don't mean for it to happen. Bias, discrimination and prejudice are not necessarily oppression, except when bias, discrimination and prejudice benefit the dominant group and damage the non-dominant group.

Four Is of oppression

There are four interconnected forms of oppressions, known as the four Is of oppression, which are unable to exist in isolation or separately from one another.

If one form of oppression is challenged, then the entire system of oppression is challenged. Every form of oppression is based on the power-oppression relational dynamic between dominant groups and non-dominant groups. The four Is of oppression (Chinook Fund, 2015) are:

1. Ideological oppression: based on an oppressive dynamic that one group is superior to another and therefore has the right to dominate the other inferior group. The dominant group in their belief to be superior attributes strengths and high value characteristics to their own group members (i.e. stronger, harder working, more intelligent and advanced) and weaknesses and low value characteristics to the members of the non-dominant group (i.e. weak, lazy, less advanced and stupid).

2. Institutional oppression: based on an oppressive dynamic that one group is superior to another and therefore has the right to control the non-dominant group, by institutionalizing laws and policies which benefit members of the dominant group to access resources and opportunities, while marginalizing and excluding members of the non-dominant group from accessing those same resources and opportunities. Whether that is intentional or unintentional exclusion, both are deemed institutional oppression.

3. Interpersonal oppression: based on an oppressive dynamic that one group is superior to another and therefore has the right to control the non-dominant group through the mistreatment, discrimination and prejudicial acts towards members of the non-dominant group by members of the dominant group (i.e. racism).

4. Internalized oppression: based on an oppressive dynamic that non-dominant group members, through their experience of being oppressed by dominant group members, now take that oppression and internalize the inferior messages towards themselves, accepting the negative, marginalizing, inferior narrative about their group and identity, and identifying with the dominant group's view of themselves and their group (i.e. holding negative stereotypes, beliefs and attitudes about themselves and their own group).

As a mirror to internalized oppression in non-dominant groups, internalized privilege or dominance can exist in members of the dominant group. This time, messages and narratives of both superiority of their own group, and the inferior status of the non-dominant group, are internalized. The beliefs of superiority and their connected privileges and benefits become normalized, leading to the denial that oppression itself exists or that the two groups are in a power-oppression relational dynamic.

Reflective exercises

Where or how do you think oppression shows up? How might it show up in relationships, in how people relate to or treat one another?

....

....

....

....

....

....

What is the result or consequence of oppression in these relationships, from the person being oppressed?

....

....

....

....

....

....

Which of your identity characteristics are oppressed (i.e. an identity that places you at the marginalized end of the spectrum of oppression)?

....

....

....

....

....

....

In what ways are these identities oppressed? What disadvantage does it give you? How do you experience oppression? (Remember that the disadvantage is the presence of a barrier.)

....

....

....

....

....

....

Which of your identity characteristics may be privileged in certain contexts but oppressed or marginalized in other contexts?

....

....

....

....

....

....

Capture any other thoughts, reactions and reflections you might have on power, privilege and oppression and working with these topics in your therapeutic practice:

....

....

....

....

....

....

Microaggressions

> **Microaggressions:** a form of daily (micro) oppression through words and actions (aggressions).

Microaggressions are verbal and behavioural assaults on a person's identity, which harm or hurt them, but may not be consciously done with intention.

The term 'micro' often gets misinterpreted or misunderstood as 'small', as if to indicate the minimal or little impact or value it holds, and therefore minimizing, dismissing or devaluing the actual oppressive aggressions being carried out on non-dominant identity members or groups. Micro refers to the everyday, continual, frequent and consistent appearance of these aggressions, without reducing, devaluing or minimizing them.

There are three forms of microaggressions (Cameron, 2020):

1. Microassaults: intentional discrimination against a perceived non-dominant group by verbalizing prejudices about the group while actively avoiding any contact with members of that group, to demean and exclude them.
2. Microinsults: intentional repeated insults, rudeness and snubbing of members of a perceived non-dominant group or criticizing something belonging to that member, to demean them and their identity.
3. Microinvalidations: dismissing, minimizing or nullifying a person's reactions to being oppressed or insulted, or their experience of being on the receiving end of someone's hostility towards them, often by claiming that their reactions are based on them being too sensitive or overreacting.

Reflective exercises

How have you experienced microaggressions towards you? What is said to you that feels dismissive and marginalizing of you because of your identity?

....

....

....

....

....

....

....

....

....

Capture any other thoughts, reactions and reflections you might have on microaggressions and what it might mean to experience them in your therapeutic practice:

....

....

....

....

....

....

....

Minority or minoritized identity

In this chapter on oppression, we have become aware of the relationship dynamic between dominant and non-dominant identity groups. For there to be a dominant majority group, there must be a non-dominant group identified as the minority. The two groups are in relationship with each other. For the dominant majority group to maintain their superiority and privileges, they must marginalize the 'other' group and position them relationally as the non-dominant 'minority' group. As it is the dominant group positioning the non-dominant group in relationship to themselves as the 'minority', the action and dynamic is of the non-dominant group being systematically marginalized and minoritized. That relationship dynamic is a system of oppression.

This has become very evident in the use of the term 'BAME' (Black and Minority Ethnic). When we unpick this term, we come to realize that it is an oppressive term based on the marginalization of and dominance over specific ethnically identified groups by the white-racialized majority identity group.

The terms 'minority' and 'minoritized' reflect and identify two different relational dynamics between the white-racialized majority identity group and Black and Brown ethnically identified groups. 'Minority' is an identity label placed on Black and Brown communities by the white-racialized dominant majority group. The label is used to identify non-white as the 'other', as a homogeneous 'minority' group, minority in number and minority at the bottom end of the power-oppression relational dynamic. 'Minority' reflects an identity of a non-dominant group, while ignoring any relationship with those doing the labelling.

When the term BAME or 'minority' becomes the label and identity of Black and Brown communities, it dismisses, denies and replaces the honour or value on those communities' history, heritage, culture, ethnicity and lived experiences. 'BAME' or 'minority' does not reflect a person's ethnicity, culture, background or heritage and in fact it does the very opposite by hiding a person's full, true and authentic identity.

For all 'BAME' organizations or organizations who state they work with 'BAME' communities, one of the most powerful ways to acknowledge the lived experiences of those very communities and their experiences of oppression and the dynamic of being 'othered' is to stop using the term 'BAME'. For minoritized groups to use the term 'BAME' is to repeat internalized oppression.

Instead, 'minoritized' reflects the relationship between the oppressors and oppressed, what is being done to a non-dominant group by the dominant identity group. 'Minoritized' labels not the community or people but the power-oppression relational dynamic of being oppressed by the dominant majority group. The label 'minoritized' identifies the relationship itself between the two groups.

Many want to relabel 'BAME' with 'global majority', but my concern with using this term is that it reduces the term down to numbers (that it is a majority in number only and not a minority). 'Global majority' misses the nuance of the relationship between oppressors and oppressed; it misses the minoritization of Black and Brown people and the knock-on effects and consequences of being minoritized, which include racism and discrimination, and being at that bottom end of the power-oppression relational dynamic and at the receiving end of the systems of oppression. Replacing 'ethnic minority' with 'global majority' eliminates, ignores, avoids and denies any of the white supremacy, dominance, oppression, power and privilege being wielded against ethnically minoritized communities.

So what would be an alternative to 'BAME'? You have two choices, either for the term to acknowledge and reflect the relationship dynamic between the dominant and non-dominant group – i.e. 'ethnically minoritized' – or labelling a group by their actual ethnicity or ethnic heritage label and identity itself (without it being the relationship between the dominant and non-dominant group), such as 'South Asian heritage'. It is a choice between focusing on reflecting the relationship dynamic itself and on the identity of the group itself and its heritage. Be clear which it is you are choosing, focusing on and identifying.

Reflective exercises

Capture any other thoughts, reactions and reflections you might have on prejudice, microaggressions and the term 'BAME' and working with these topics in your therapeutic practice:

....

....

....

....

....

....

Is this a topic you need to gain more understanding of or read more about? If so, make a note of what questions you might have:

....

....

....

....

....

....

CHAPTER 10

White Privilege

> **White privilege:** presence of an unearned advantage or benefit as well as the absence of a disadvantage, barrier or impediment for members of the dominant white-racialized group.

The presence of an advantage and the absence of a disadvantage are not mutually exclusive. They can exist simultaneously. Privilege can show up as daily experiences, often taken for granted and unnoticed, which offer ease for that person to navigate daily life.

White privilege has been described using the metaphor of 'an invisible weightless knapsack of special provisions, maps, passports, codebooks, visas, clothes, tools and blank checks' (McIntosh, 1989, p.63). These are the presence of benefits and absence of barriers, which can be taken advantage of, to succeed in life, by those of a white-racialized identity.

White privilege is the privilege experienced at the dominant end of the racial system of oppression by those of a white-racialized identity. It is the privilege to not experience racially based discrimination and racism, to not experience being at the oppressed end of the racial system of oppression, and so not experience marginalization, minimization or oppression because of their dominant racialized identity. It is to experience whiteness as the dominant identity and therefore 'normative' identity, not to be othered or seen as 'minority'. To learn more about the racial system of oppression, see Chapter 6.

White privilege, as with all types of dominant identity characteristics, can show up as personal, societal and institutional privileges, such as opportunities, choices, entitlements, responsibilities and positive assumptions, projections and expectations about that identity group. Being a member of the dominant majority group means the social system is created for you, works in your favour and automatically gives you unearned benefits (white privilege) because of your membership. It offers you structural advantages and benefits while ensuring that disadvantages or barriers are absent. For an introduction to privilege as a wider topic, please see Chapter 8.

For example, white privilege can show up as a person of white-racialized identity safely sharing an opinion, without it representing their racialized identity or ethnicity. It doesn't define their image or identity, it doesn't jeopardize their job, there is no risk of being shut down, cancelled or dismissed. This is a daily and taken-for-granted privilege white-racialized people have, while racially marginalized and minoritized people need to double-check and do a quick risk assessment of the impact and jeopardy before sharing their opinion.

At a systemic level, the racial system of oppression supports the dominant white identity to hold positions of power and influence, to be able to create social, structural and cultural policies and practices. This ultimately works to set up and maintain a society that benefits the dominant white identity and keeps that identity in a position of supremacy and power (Thomas, 2022).

Reflective exercises

How do you feel in reading about white privilege and structural advantages and disadvantages?

....

....

....

....

....

How are you triggered when reflecting on privilege through the racial lens and spectrum of oppression?

....

....

....

....

....

To identify and help people assess the many ways in which they may experience white privilege, Peggy McIntosh (1989) created the now famous 'unpacking the invisible knapsack' exercise. It is a list of daily experiences, which you could 'tick' if you experienced them. These 'daily experiences' were in fact examples of white privilege, which if experienced, highlighted the degree to which they were embedded in daily life and taken for granted.

When this exercise is done in a group of diverse ethnically racialized members, what becomes evident is that the white racially identified members experience these 'daily experiences' (white privileges) whereas the Black and Brown racially identified members do not experience them.

Below are listed some of those daily experiences, taken from McIntosh's (1989) 'knapsack' exercise:

- I am never asked to speak for all the people of my racial group.
- I can easily buy posters, postcards, picture books, greeting cards, dolls, toys and children's magazines featuring people of my race.
- I can turn on the television or open to the front page of the paper and see people of my race widely represented.
- I can criticize our government and talk about how much I fear its policies and behaviour without being seen as a cultural outsider.
- I can be sure that if I need legal or medical help, my race will not work against me.
- When I am told about our national heritage or 'civilization' I am shown that people of my colour made it what it is.
- I can choose blemish cover or bandages in 'flesh' colour and have them more or less match my skin.
- I can be sure that my children will be given curricular materials that testify to the existence of their race.

Reflective exercises

What are your immediate reactions and thoughts to this list and to the 'knapsack' exercise?

....

....

....

....

....

....

Identify four unearned advantages that you experience because of your racialized identity:

....

....

....

....

....

....

Identify four unearned advantages that you experience because of any other dominant identity characteristic (also name which identity characteristic gives you this advantage):

....

....

....

....

....

....

Identify four unearned disadvantages that you experience because of your racialized identity:

....

....

....

....

....

....

Identify four unearned disadvantages that you experience because of any other non-dominant identity characteristic (also name which identity characteristic gives you this disadvantage):

....

....

....

....

....

....

How do you feel when you reflect on your privileged and disadvantaged experiences that you have just identified? What are you triggered by and how do you want to respond to your answers?

....

....

....

....

....

....

If you hold white privilege, it is important to sit with how you feel but this does not mean only to sit with how you feel and experience it. Otherwise in just looking at yourself, you are avoiding perhaps the more challenging feelings and experiences of those who don't hold your white privilege. You need to be able to look at both your own and other people's experiences. This is where holding on to 'two truths' becomes additionally important. You need to be able to hold both truths in mind: those with and those without white privilege.

Of course, it is also important to remember that you can hold both privilege *and* oppression in your own identity, that parts of your identity hold privilege while at the same time, other parts of your identity get oppressed and marginalized. So, 'two truths' can co-exist within your own identity as well as between you and another person.

Reflective exercises

Capture any other thoughts, reactions and reflections you might have on white privilege and working with this topic in your therapeutic practice:

....

....

....

....

....

....

Is this a topic you need to gain more understanding of or read more about? If so, make a note of what questions you might have:

....

....

....

....

....

....

CHAPTER 11

Landscapes, Safe Spaces and Belonging

Landscapes: the social, cultural, structural, systemic, political, historical, generational, geographical and relational environment we exist in.

Safe spaces: a space and/or group in which a person can feel safe in, and show up fully and authentically, without being on the receiving end of any oppression, discrimination, prejudice or exclusion.

Belonging: feeling included, safe, a part of and fully accepted in a space or group and being able to show up in a full and authentic identity, without the need to be or do something additional to be accepted.

Before we look further at what we understand by the terms 'landscapes', 'safe spaces' and 'belonging', I would like to invite you to participate in an activity, which I call the 'Street Map' exercise. I will walk you through the four-step process of this exercise below.

Reflective exercise

Street Map exercise
Step 1: Draw a street map of a regular journey you take, such as your commute to work, trip to the supermarket, the school run, any journey which is a familiar and regular journey you take. This journey can be on any form of transport or walking; it does not need to be in the car.

Step 2: Add to your map by answering the following questions:

- What is in your environment when you take this journey?
- What do you see around you?
- What buildings, landmarks, monuments, shops, houses, gardens or green spaces do you see? Is there a canal or body of water? What do you notice that is in your environment?
- What type of transport are you using? Or are you walking? Is it a direct journey or do you stop on the way, for example for a coffee?
- Is anyone with you? Who else do you notice on your journey? What identities or communities (racial, ethnic, faith, cultural) do you often see or are represented on your journey?

Add any of the above to your map.

Step 3: Now reflect on the map you have drawn and your experience of the journey through a series of questions: How do you feel and experience the journey? What are you feeling as you take this journey? Do your feelings change depending on whereabouts you are in the journey? Is the journey peaceful, stressful or rushed, or do you take your time? Is it enjoyable or not?

....

....

....

....

....

....

Step 4: Does the journey feel safe to you? Are there parts of the journey that feel unsafe? If so, which parts? Do you feel that you belong in the spaces where your journey takes place? If yes or no, why might that be? What perhaps feels threatening or worrying about the space your journey takes place in?

....

....

....

....

....

....

Step 5: What is referenced or included in it? How does your map and experience of the journey reflect your cultural identity and lived experience? Does your map reflect a diversity of identities or communities, or does it reflect a more homogeneous identity or community? What else influenced your map and your journey? Does your ethnicity, faith, age or gender influence the journey you take and how you experience it?

....

....

....

....

....

....

Step 6: In looking at your answers above, what are your reflections, feelings and thoughts about how your journey reflects who you are? What are your thoughts on any link between your journey's experience, the landscape and your feelings of safety and belonging, or a lack of safety and not belonging? What has surprised you about what your map reveals about you and why?

....

....

....

....

....

....

There is a relationship between the landscape and our identity, which results in how we experience the external world and if it feels safe to us and if we feel we belong in that space. In your answers to the previous questions, were you able to spot any relationship between the landscape, your identity and how you experience that space?

Being in a space doesn't automatically make you feel safe, that you belong, that you are welcomed there, are seen as an equal and are being included. Belonging is not the same as attending or turning up in a space. To feel included does not mean the same as belonging. Inclusion is to be allowed into the space or have access to the space. Belonging is to feel fully accepted, to show up in a full and authentic identity, without the need to be or do something additional to be accepted, to be part of the space or group, to be there.

Spaces may be accessible but that doesn't make them safe. Spaces may want to include you but that doesn't mean you belong. This applies to social, cultural, professional, geographical and relational space. To all spaces. And for those 'in charge' of these spaces, it is not always understood or recognized how they are gatekeeping these spaces, owning them as their own, and so creating barriers as to who gets let in, who feels safe once in and how they relate to people in the space to support them in feeling that they belong there.

It is a privilege to be able to access spaces without considering or worrying if you will feel safe or if you belong in that space. You just turn up. You see other people, who represent a shared identity, sharing that space with you. A marker of belonging, a marker to indicate that 'we' in our shared identity can be here, can feel this space is available to us and that we belong. At the other end of the spectrum, it is an oppression, a marginalization, if you do worry and if you do have to think or question beforehand, will I feel safe there? Will I feel included and that I belong there? Is the space for me? Will I be the only one (of my ethnicity, faith, race, gender)? Will I be represented by other people in that space or by the people in that event's speaker line-up or panel? Or will I again be minoritized?

This is because inclusion and belonging are two power dynamics at play, in how we are being related to. On a belonging continuum, at one end is 'belonging' where the majority identity sits, and at the other end is 'outsider', where the minority identity sits. Where we are on that spectrum depends on where our identity falls on the majority or minority end of the spectrum, and therefore if we belong or don't belong in that space. If we are in the majority/dominant identity group, we belong in the space. If we are in the minority/outsider identity group, we don't belong in that space, even if we have access or are included in being in the space itself. Being in the space, being included, does not mean that relationally we are being related to equally, represented equally or considered in the space. We can be physically present (included) in a space but that doesn't automatically mean we belong there. There is, of course, another situation which can be experienced and that is both not being included and not feeling you belong, which leaves you being excluded completely from that space. The gatekeeping of the space by the dominant majority group can mean that a minoritized individual doesn't even get access to the space.

Reflective exercises

Reflecting on the previous map exercise and what emerged for you, what are your experiences of belonging and being in external safe spaces? Are safe spaces commonly available to you or are they hard to find?

....

....

....

....

....

Where do you feel you belong? What places, spaces, locations, groups or people are your belonging and safe spaces?

....

....

....

....

....

....

What parts of your identity are being acknowledged or not acknowledged in safe spaces where you feel you belong? What do you need for a space to feel safe for you?

....

....

....

....

....

....

Where is not safe? Where do you feel you don't belong? What spaces do you attend or turn up in but don't feel you belong? What are the fearful aspects of unsafe spaces?

....

....

....

....

....

....

What parts of your identity are being acknowledged or not acknowledged in unsafe spaces where you feel you don't belong? What is not being met and seen in you or what needs are not being met to make you feel unsafe?

....

....

....

....

....

....

What spaces have changed for you, either from safe to unsafe, or from unsafe to safe? And why, what has made that change happen for you?

....

....

....

....

....

....

How do your experiences of safe spaces and feelings of belonging relate to your identity and intersectionality?

....

....

....

....

....

....

Capture any other thoughts, reactions and reflections you might have on your relationship with the external landscape and experiences of safe/unsafe spaces and belonging and working with these topics in your therapeutic practice:

....

....

....

....

....

....

Is this a topic you need to gain more understanding of or read more about? If so, make a note of what questions you might have:

....

....

....

....

....

....

Part 2: Reflections

Looking back at your initial barriers or challenges at the beginning of this section, how have they changed for you?

....

....

....

....

....

....

Looking back at your initial reactions to learning about intersectionality, power, privilege or oppression, what has your experience been to learn about these topics? How was your experience different from how you expected it to be? Did anything surprise you?

....

....

....

....

....

....

Do you still perceive, or can you identify, any barriers? If so, what are the barriers or challenges remaining?

....

....

....

....

....

....

Capture any other thoughts, reactions and reflections you might have on anything we have covered in Part 2 and working with these topics in your therapeutic practice:

....

....

....

....

....

....

Working within Diversity in Therapeutic Practice

In Part 3, I will present the application of the Working within Diversity model and its five components to therapeutic practice and what we need to consider to be able to offer an anti-oppressive approach and practice.

The Working within Diversity model (Figure 15) outlines five components to working in an anti-oppressive practice and approach:

Component 1: Structural and Systemic Context of Counselling

Component 2: Identity and Intersectionality (of counsellor and client)

Component 3: Power

Component 4: Therapeutic Relationship (in therapy and supervision)

Component 5: Therapeutic Process (in therapy and supervision)

Figure 15: Working within Diversity model (with five components of model)

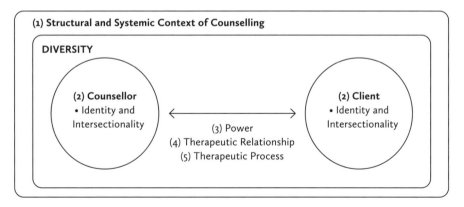

How do you develop anti-oppressive practice?

In applying the Working within Diversity model within your therapeutic relationships and the therapeutic process, you will be able to consider how each of its five components impact and influence the process and relationships, and how you can ensure you are aiming to flatten the power, to offer a process and relationship which does not oppress your clients or supervisees.

We will be working our way through each of the five components in the following chapters (Chapters 12–16). However, it is important to recognize that the five components are part of the whole therapeutic process and relationship, and so are interconnected and work together, impacting and influencing one another as well as the entire therapeutic process and relationship. We can't think about one component without considering the other four (see Figure 16).

Figure 16: Working within Diversity: the five interconnected components in anti-oppressive practice

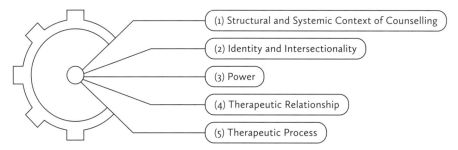

Throughout Part 3, you will be invited to think about your own role in your work, as well as your clients'. For the purposes of engaging in the activities and reflective exercises, I invite you to think of a current or recent client, as a case study, to help support your learning. You may even wish to choose two case study clients, who present with different intersectional identities, to help further your understanding of how this model can be applied to your therapeutic and clinical practice.

Before we start to look at the five components, let's think about what you imagine anti-oppressive practice would look like. This can be based on what you've read in previous chapters or what you have learned elsewhere in previous trainings and reading on the subject, or what you imagine it would look like.

Reflective exercises

Imagine you are the counselling client; what would you want from your counsellor, to feel that they are offering you an anti-oppressive counselling practice and therapeutic relationship? How would you know it was anti-oppressive? What would they be saying or doing and how would they be facilitating the process? What would be the signs of an anti-oppressive practice?

....

....

....

....

....

....

How would the counsellor be approaching you to establish a relationship? What would the relationship look and feel like? What do you imagine the assessment process to look and feel like? What else would you consider to be part of an anti-oppressive approach? What would you want or need your counsellor to know about you, for them to be able to offer you anti-oppressive counselling?

....

....

....

....

....

....

Now as the counsellor, what factors or aspects within your process and therapeutic relationships would you need to consider to offer anti-oppressive counselling?

....

....

....

....

....

....

In thinking of your chosen case study client, what, at this stage, might you need to add, change or adjust in your current work with the client?

....

....

....

....

....

....

Based on your answers to the previous questions, what do you think, at this stage, you might need to change or adjust in your current overall practice? What might you now need to add, adjust or take away from your current practice?

....

....

....

....

....

....

CHAPTER 12

Component 1: Structural and Systemic Context of Counselling

For an introduction on the topic of external structural and systemic contexts, see Chapters 7–10.

Counselling does not exist in a vacuum. The profession and its therapeutic practice sit inside the external 'out there' systemic, structural, social, cultural, political, historical contexts of society. Therefore, when we acknowledge that social injustices, inequalities, privileges and oppression exist in society ('out there') we can acknowledge that the profession sits inside this, and is shaped by this systemic and structural context, which is then embedded into the profession and practice ('in here'). Therapy is systemically, structurally, politically, culturally, historically and socially located.

By acknowledging the systemic and structural context of counselling, we can start to acknowledge how the therapeutic work and practice are shaped by systemic inequality, which unconsciously supports or repeats a power-oppressive relational dynamic with clients. These systems of oppression can be re-enacted, for example a dominant counsellor and non-dominant client in therapeutic relationship with one another.

Anti-oppressive practice is an integral part of ethical practice, explicitly acknowledging structural and systemic inequalities, systems of oppression and power-oppression relational dynamics. We can understand its structural presence and influence on the profession, on the 'in here' process and therapeutic relationships. It supports our understanding of the systemic and structural context of our and our clients' lived experiences, which end of systems of oppression and power-oppression relational dynamics we each sit at, and therefore how to work with it, how it appears and how it gets repeated and played out 'in here'.

When working with clients through an intersectional lens, we can recognize their full intersectional identity. This includes how the client, and their lived experience, is impacted by inequality and social hostility. We can explore how a client relates to their own identity, lived experiences and experiences of privilege and oppression 'out there', while exploring how all this impacts on the work in counselling 'in here'. By recognizing and holding simultaneously the 'two truths' of our client's identity and lived experiences and our own, we can examine our own biases and prejudices and how they impact on the work and therapeutic relationship.

Using an intersectional lens to understand that the work 'in here' takes place in the space of the relationship between two people (two intersectional identities), we can recognize how each is impacting on the other and on the relationship. The process emerges because of the two people in the room, who they are and how they relate to one another, which is all influenced by their own identity and lived experiences, contained within the multiple 'out there' contexts.

This practice asks us to look not only at the external 'out there' system or clients but calls on us to do the work on ourselves first. What changes do we need to make to ourselves? Our worldview is shaped by a systemically, structurally, culturally, socially, politically, historically determined lens. How we see the world is shaped through that lens. That lens is shaped by our experience in the systemic and structural context of the world, its societies, cultures, politics. It is important to understand how we are shaped by our context and lived experience in that context. What lens are you seeing the world through and what lens is the client seeing the world through?

In wearing systemic and intersectional lenses through which to look at our practice, we must also look at ourselves and take up a position of cultural attunement (cultural humility, cultural empathy and cultural curiosity). This is an ongoing process and practice for us and not a competency 'finish line' to reach and get over. It is a commitment to understanding our own identity and lived experience, shaped by the systemic and structural context, which is being brought into our practice, process and therapeutic relationships we are offering and facilitating for our clients.

To offer cultural humility is to be respectful of people's experience of systemic inequalities and their social locations. It is to acknowledge and accept all the spectrums, including the power and privilege experienced by dominant identities, and to understand that it's about how our identity and lived experiences are shaped by our location, context and relationships with systemic and structural contexts of inequality and oppression. Cultural humility asks us to take up a position of humility and non-judgement to everyone and the diverse lived experiences they have had.

To offer cultural empathy is to take up a position of openness and willingness to see the client fully, their intersectionality, their experiences of power, privilege or oppression, their lived experiences within systemic and structural inequality. It is to empathize with their experiences, to be willing to feel and be affected by their lived experience and to sit with, honour and value and hold 'two truths' of identity and lived experiences, that of yours and your client's.

To offer cultural curiosity is to approach our work and clients from a position of curiosity and interest, to understand their identity, their lived experiences and to allow the work to unfold from a place of 'not knowing', not having the answers, not needing to fix or give advice, but to offer the space for the client to make meaning themselves of their lived experiences.

We need to be aware of what is stopping us from doing this work individually ourselves (i.e. internal barriers) and in our organizations (i.e. policies/procedures, what support we need in our organizations). You need to know your own barriers and resistances to doing this work; to understand what you find challenging and difficult. You may need to look at uncomfortable parts of your identity, inter-sectionality or the impact and influence of systems of oppression on your lived experiences.

Reflective exercises

What is your current understanding of the systemic context and cultural, social, political impact on your work? What role do they play? What is the impact of the systemic and structural context on you? What is the impact on your clients? Do you consider a systemic, cultural, social or political impact on your client's work?

....

....

....

....

....

....

In thinking of your case study client, how might you now view the client through the systemic, cultural, social or political lens? How might you contextualize your client's experience within this external context? How does your client experience the 'out there'?

....

....

....

....

....

....

How might the client be experiencing systems of oppression? In what ways do they experience oppression? Where might they experience power and privilege? How is your client impacted by systemic and structural inequality? How might this change how you see the client's issues or presenting problem?

....

....

....

....

....

....

How, and in what ways, is the client's experience of the 'out there' different or like yours? Do you both experience the same or different types of privilege or oppression?

....

....

....

....

....

....

Where and how might both of your experiences of the 'out there' power-oppressive relational dynamic get replayed and repeated 'in here'?

....

....

....

....

....

....

What else about the 'out there' context do you now need to consider in working with your client? What else 'out there' will impact on your work and relationship together?

....

....

....

....

....

....

CHAPTER 13

Component 2: Identity and Intersectionality

In this chapter, we will explore the identity and intersectionality of both counsellor and client and what to look for and identify within the component to be able to work within diversity. For an introduction on the topic of identity and intersectionality, see Chapter 7.

'Working within diversity' directly acknowledges that there are two unique identities in the room, which are in relationship with one another. Both the client and counsellor are seen for their own unique intersectional identities, and that the relationship which unfolds between the two of them does so because of these two unique intersectional identities. Both identities co-exist and so they are not mutually exclusive (see Figure 17).

The principle of 'two identities' and there being two truths simultaneously existing (see Chapter 2 for a detailed account of this principle) is central to 'working within diversity', because it locates the identities of both the counsellor and the client in relationship with one another at the heart of the work. Two identities, and therefore, two truths, in relationship with one another. This positions both identities within the structural and systemic context of counselling (Component 1) (see Chapter 12 for an explanation of Component 1).

Figure 17: Two identities (and two truths) in the room and in therapeutic relationship

Tool: Identity Wheel

The Identity Wheel (Figures 3 and 4) supports exploring the depth and breadth of identity characteristics of the counsellor and client being brought into the counselling room and therefore highlights what characteristics are impacting on the counselling process and therapeutic relationship. The Identity Wheel template (Figure 4) is useful to fill out for yourself and for each client, to be able to identify the specific identity characteristics and the combination of characteristics present in your therapeutic relationships.

There is both an Identity Wheel tool with the identity characteristics labelled (Figure 3) and a blank Identity Wheel tool (Figure 4) template in the online Appendix for you to be able to download and fill out. See Chapter 3 for more information about the Identity Wheel itself.

Identity of counsellor

Understanding the external concepts of identity, intersectionality, systems of oppression and the embedded relationship between dominant and non-dominant groups in society (covered in Part 2) is crucial to understanding what underpins the two identities in the therapy room.

The counsellor's identity is not a blank slate or 'neutral'. The counsellor's identity is present, proactive and holds a value. It offers a diversity of identity. In the same way, the client also offers a diversity of identity. Both identities are fully present in the room and in the relationship. Our visible identity as the counsellor – our ethnicity, gender, faith, age, ability or disability – can't be removed, dismissed, ignored or made invisible. It's how we understand its impact and work with it that matters.

We need to recognize that we self-identify (whether consciously or unconsciously) all our identity characteristics (as listed in the Identity Wheel tool, Figure 3), while at the same time others are also identifying and labelling our identity, this being a perceived identity projected onto us. Our identity is reacted, related and responded to, consciously and unconsciously, by the client.

Our identity (or an identity characteristic), as the counsellor, may be the reason why clients choose us as their therapist. This is often because the client believes this identity or identity characteristic will help them to feel understood, recognized and welcomed into the therapeutic relationship and space. This need of the client is important to recognize, honour and value.

Our own identity, as we have seen from the Identity Wheel, not only includes visible and physical characteristics, but also our worldview, which has been shaped through our interpersonal relationships, beliefs and values, cultural, political, religious and social views and our lived experiences in the context of systemic and structural inequalities.

We also hold our own beliefs, values and attitudes in relation to our identity characteristics, such as who we are ethnically, racially, culturally, religiously and so on, which creates a deeply held approach to how we show up in the world, how we think, are, do, relate, interact and live.

Our identity, and all that underpins it, is what is enacted, brought to and related with in our relationships, both 'out there' in society and 'in here' in the therapy room with our clients. Recognizing the impact of our identity on relationships is important, so that we do not misuse our power or re-create any oppressive relationship or relational dynamic in our therapeutic relationships with our clients.

The challenge then is to identify our identity and what the impact might be in our work and in our attitudes towards our clients and the diversity of identities we work with.

Reflective exercises

Using your completed Identity Wheel (Chapter 3, Figure 4), as a counsellor, what parts of your identity are visible in the room for you? What parts of your identity are seen by clients? What impact does this have on your work?

....

....

....

....

....

....

In thinking of your case study client, what has been the impact or influence of your identity on your work with this client? Did the client choose you, and, if so, why? Was it to do with your identity? What were they expecting from you? What assumptions did they make about you?

....

....

....

....

....

....

What impact or influence do you think your cultural, racialized or ethnic identity has on your attitude towards your work, your clients or the presenting problems/ issues they bring into session? What impact has this had on the work with your case study client?

....

....

....

....

....

....

What are some assumptions, stereotypes and biases made about you, based on your identity, by clients and/or your case study client? What impact might that have on you or has it had on you? What impact has it had on your case study client and on your therapeutic relationship?

....

....

....

....

....

....

Do your clients choose you as their counsellor because of a particular identity characteristic or category which you belong to (and is either consciously or unconsciously known by the client)? What is the impact of that characteristic on your work and on your therapeutic relationships? What assumptions, stereotypes or biases do your clients make about you, based on that identity characteristic?

....

....

....

....

....

....

Identity of client

For the client, as with ourselves, there is the self-identity of the client (how they identify themselves) and there is also the perceived identity of the client by us as the counsellor.

Let's explore what impact or effect this might have.

Activity: Complete an 'Identity Wheel' for your case study client (Figure 4). A template of the Identity Wheel is provided in the online Appendix, which you can download and use for this activity. Use the completed Identity Wheel (Figure 3) as a prompt for the categories of identity characteristics.

Having completed the Identity Wheel for your case study client, reflect on the following questions:

- What parts of your client's identity are visible in the room for you?
- What are some assumptions, stereotypes and biases you have made about this client, based on their visible identity?
- What impact might that have on you working with the client and on the therapeutic relationship?
- What else does the Identity Wheel reveal to you about your client's identity?
- How does the Identity Wheel help you understand your client?
- What are you now aware of about the client and their identity that you were not aware of before?

- What fears do you have in working with this client?
- What do you need to consider in your work with them?
- What do your answers reveal or highlight to you?

You can also use your client's Identity Wheel to see how the wheel gets added to or changed over the process of working together. Do you identify or label the client in a way that is different from how the client self-identifies? If so, why might that be?

Throughout the rest of this chapter we will be looking at some of these identity characteristics in more detail.

Internal world of the client

The client's worldview, lived experiences, relationships, sense of who they are in the world and their meaning-making of all of these are embedded in their identity.

Holding the space and containing the client's material doesn't automatically mean that we are being emotionally available and empathizing with their material, experiences and identity.

To enter the client's world, particularly their internal world of emotions and lived experiences, we are inviting ourselves to enter a different world from our own. It is the equivalent of walking through the wardrobe and into Narnia. We are entering a world with no map, or no reference points (at this stage) and it is for us to sit with, hold, empathize and facilitate the processing of their life in their world. In the client sharing their narrative with us, they are holding up the map, and while the client points out and shares parts of the map with us, we are exploring the map together. We are looking to understand the client's map, lived experiences and worldview in the context of their intersectional identity (part of Component 2 – identity) within the external 'out there' social context (Component 1 – external contexts), while at the same time recognizing that by being in the client's world, we are influencing how the client presents their map, how they feel about us entering their world and the experience of our relationship in their world (part of Components 3, 4 and 5 – power, therapeutic relationship and therapeutic process).

There may be a fear of bringing those experiences back with you through the wardrobe because you can't forget what you've seen or heard. There may be a fear that it may challenge your own sense of self, that what you see in your client's world can challenge or change your own view of your experiences, which impacts on your own map and internal world.

The challenge to working as a counsellor is to build the emotional capacity and courage to enter Narnia (the client's world) and be prepared to sit with the unknown and your own anxiety of sitting and staying there, without wanting to run back through the wardrobe. This comes from moving into a position of openness, curiosity and empathy.

Culture

For an introduction on the topic of culture, see Chapter 4.

Often when we think about a client's culture or 'working with culture' or 'working cross-culturally', we fall into the same trap as 'cultural competence', that being a cognitive-, knowledge-, subject-based understanding of culture. It is something learned through research, or worse by asking your client for explanations or being taught about their 'culture', and then assessing how well you 'know' about a client's culture, rather than their actual experience of their culture and what it means for them (see Chapter 2 on cultural attunement for further explanations on the problem of cultural 'competence').

Instead, we need to move to a position of being culturally attuned towards a client's culture and look to the client's understanding, experience, exploration and reflections on how they view their culture and how it influences, impacts, affects and shows up for them, in their everyday, in their worldview lens and in how they relate to us, the counsellor, in the therapeutic relationship. We are attuning to the client and their cultural context (see Chapter 2 for further details on the principle of cultural attunement).

Part of practising and being culturally attuned is to understand and approach culture as a framework and context for our clients' lived experience as well as it being part of their identity, as culture exists both externally and internally in each person. For example, the collectivist and individualist culture framework and culturally close and culturally distant framework (explored below) can help to support us in being attuned to the client's cultural context. This helps facilitate the process of how the client explores and makes meaning of their lived experiences, relationships and sense of self/identity, which will be present in the work and our therapeutic relationship with the client.

Collectivist and individualist cultures

For an introduction to the topic of collectivist and individualist culture, see Chapter 4.

Collectivist and individualist cultures form an aspect of the cultural framework, context and identity for our clients and so we can explore how this may influence how clients express their concerns, what their expectations, goals and experiences in counselling might be and how they relate to the counselling process and counsellor in the therapeutic relationship.

For the individualist client, where independence and self-sufficiency are valued, and where boundaries are around an individual sense of self, they may be more able to prioritize their personal ethics and comfort, and their individual or own issues that they bring to counselling. They are more likely to prioritize their needs, identify what their goals are in counselling and what they want to individually achieve from counselling by the end of it. This can often be a good, complementary match for Western counselling as its modalities are born out of individualist cultures that encourage self-exploration and self-determination.

Counselling or counsellors may be unfamiliar to a client from a collectivist culture who understands their relational dynamics and sense of self through being part of a group, family and culture. For the collectivist client, the one-on-one therapeutic relationship could be experienced as a very exclusive and intense relationship. The counsellor metaphorically may experience themselves not in an 'individualist' therapeutic relationship with the client but in a 'collectivist' therapeutic relationship with the client, who is connected to the rest of their collective community or family. Clients talk about themselves in the context of their family, and they don't regard themselves as having an individual identity but instead they are wife, husband, mother, father, son, daughter, brother, sister, daughter-in-law, son-in-law and so on. Their sense of self is expressed in relation to others. This can be felt as if there are many people in the room with the client. The client brings into the room the rest of their family who make up their sense of self as a 'we'. When working with these clients, a good question to ask yourself is, 'who is in the room?' Not only will it feel as if there are a lot of people if they are a collectivist 'we' client, but it can also help you to attune to whether your client is individualist or collectivist.

Collectivist cultures and groups are community based, so they often look for advice and practical solutions, and may treat the counsellor as if they were a doctor or faith leader. In looking for solutions, advice or answers, they can approach the counselling in the same way that they may approach a medical appointment. This can look like them sharing with you all their problems (symptoms), for you to listen to and then at the end for you to give them your opinion, advice or solutions, like an 'emotional prescription'. What can often support a collectivist client to engage in counselling is for them to have an explanation of the counselling process, how the space is to be used and what you as the counsellor will facilitate in the space for them to explore their experiences. Sometimes we need to be clear and explicit that we don't offer advice or solutions.

Collectivist cultures lay greater emphasis on norms and authority and are greatly concerned with group loyalty and cohesion. The priority is the family, with a strong emphasis on duty to the family. An individual's responsibility and duty are to the family before the self. Individual desires and needs are sacrificed for the good of the group. Family well-being is fostered by cooperation, mutual dependency, sacrifice, loyalty and conforming to expected roles and boundaries. Loyalty, obedience to parents and conformity to cultural norms and family expectations is required. Social consciousness is related to a high regard for learning, as education leads to success, and success is measured by the ability to take care of the family and to give back to the community. This may impact the result, outcome or goal that the client is looking for in counselling, because are they looking for an outcome or solution as to how they can conform to their group's cultural norms and meet the expectations placed on them?

As the client's understanding of self is as a 'we', this may also impact on their ability to access help, feel empowered during the process and have a sense of achievable change. Accessing counselling may be felt as a failure to live up to their cultural expectations or fulfil their role within their community.

The collectivist nature of the family affects the individual concept of the client as an independent person. As there is no 'I', there is less individual choice, autonomy or independence, as these would be seen as in direct conflict with the client's culture, family relationships and role within family. The client may come to counselling because of this very conflict between their wish for autonomy as an individual 'I' and the pressure or expectation to stay within their collectivist 'we' identity and cultural role. Whatever the issue may be that that client is bringing to counselling, the question to ask is, 'what is a choice for the client? What choices are available to them and what choices are not?' This will help us to identify what level of autonomy the client has and in what areas of their life.

In addition to considering a client's (or your own) collectivist or individualist culture, we also need to consider the historical and generational influence on their culture. For example, second, third or any following generation may have a history or heritage of a collectivist culture but may have adapted to, internalized and experienced an individualistic culture due to migration or a change in their external environment, society and culture. We need to consider if a client holds a historical, generational and personal experience of culture that is of both individualistic and collectivist cultures. We can explore how this is experienced by the client in holding in mind both cultures and the potential impact on their sense of self and identity, while recognizing how it may show up in the therapeutic process, outcomes and relationship.

The following questions can help support you to understand and explore the client's cultural context. Some of the questions are prompts for you to ask yourself to help you reflect on the client's culture. Others are questions to be asked of your client, either during an assessment or sessions, as you deem appropriate for them.

Please note that all the suggested questions listed in the below 'tools' are intended to be asked in a manner which holds these questions lightly and inquisitively rather than as prescriptive and mandatory.

Tool: Culture questions

Identity and family:

- Is the client an 'I' or 'we'? How do they talk about their sense of self? As an individual or in relation to others?
- Have they experienced both individualist and collectivist cultures? Do they hold a combination of both a 'we' and 'I' sense of self depending on their environment and who they are with?
- What is their family tree or relationship structure?
- What is their family's generational culture? Is this as a 'we' or 'I'?
- What is the quality of their relationships? Who is significant for the client?
- Are these family members supportive or unsupportive of the client?
- Who else do they live with? Is there an extended family set-up within the home?
- What are the expectations for living at home and while being at home?
- What are the expectations on the client regarding family and marriage?
- How fixed is the client's understanding, duty and obligation to fulfil their cultural roles and expectations?
- What level of autonomy does the client have? What might be the impact or influence in here and on their expectations of goals and change?
- Who else is metaphorically showing up in the room? Does the client focus on other people and their relationship with those people?
- What is the client's cultural and generational history? Does the client come from, or have they experienced or had a generational experience of historical trauma or oppression?
- What is their political status? Do they identify as a refugee, asylum seeker, immigrant, born from previous generational immigration (historical immigration)?
- How is the issue/presenting problem they are bringing to counselling related to their culture and family?
- Is the issue linked to honour and shame? Is it part of an honour code?

Social:

- What social support does the client have around them?
- Are they from the same or similar cultural identity as the client or culturally distant from the client?
- Does the client have opportunity to meet with people from their same cultural, ethnic or faith identity?

Study/Employment:

- What is the client's current employment/education status?
- Are there culturally, ethnically or faith-close identified employees that the client works or studies with? Does the client feel supported by them?
- Is there any sensitivity to culture or faith demonstrated by their employer/teachers?
- If not employed, are they able to meet with people in their community who are close to them in terms of culture or faith?
- What are the expectations on the client regarding education and work?

Honour and shame

For an introduction to the topic of honour and shame, see Chapter 4.

When we think about honour codes and shame, we can start to see the parallel with clients from collectivist 'we' cultures. This is because honour codes are embedded in collectivist groups and dynamics. As honour is shared among the family it means that the actions and behaviours of one person in that group reflect the entire group. Honour codes can therefore be in direct conflict with the client's individual needs. A lack of awareness of family honour could unintentionally lead to additional conflict by supporting an individualist culture's values and codes of autonomy, independency and self-sufficiency. Counselling must work within the client's collectivist 'we' culture.

When honour codes are broken, the shame of it is held by that individual. When the shame is brought into the counselling room it is often heavy, often difficult to disclose and the counsellor can also be the first or only person to whom the client has spoken about it.

The nature of shame being internally held by the client means that it is often a heavy burden that the client is carrying alone. The fear of sharing the shame in counselling is the assumption, expectation or projection that the counsellor will side with collectivist culture's values and beliefs in upholding the honour and further shame the client. As a counsellor, what is important to understand and demonstrate when working with shame is your understanding of shame within the honour code, your empathy to the shame being internally and individually held by the client, and the ripple effect and impact on the client's collectivist family relationships and dynamics and how they may have changed because of the shame.

Faith, beliefs and spirituality

For an introduction to the topic of faith, beliefs and spirituality, see Chapter 5.

In counselling, our professional frame of reference consists of theory, a framework, the therapeutic frame, and we work within the boundary of guidance, of best practice and of an ethical framework, which includes values, ethics, principles and morals.

When working with clients and needing to consider their faith, beliefs and spirituality, it can seem incredibly overwhelming to feel that you need to know everything about a particular religion or faith. Where do you start in understanding all the beliefs, relationship dynamics, practices and traditions? One way to help us not feel overwhelmed is to recognize the parallels between the ethical framework of counselling and the ethical framework of your client's faith, beliefs or spiritual practice.

One approach on how to enter the frame of reference of your client's faith, belief or spirituality is to identify the boundaries, guidance, values, ethics, principles and morals of their faith. This can be an important part of their assessment process.

The following questions can be included in the assessment to help both you and your client to identify the client's faith, beliefs and spirituality, and their individual relationship with it, and how this may influence or be related to what the client brings to counselling to work on.

Tool: Faith, beliefs and spirituality assessment questions

- What gives you hope? What keeps you going in life?
- Is there a faith, religion, spiritual practice or belief system that you identify with?
- Do you have any faith, religion, spiritual practice or beliefs which are important to you?

- How does this support you? How is this part of your self-care practice?
- Does your spiritual or faith practice make you feel uneasy about any aspect of this counselling practice or process?
- How does your spirituality affect you? Does it make you feel loved/accepted/belonging or isolated/alone, and so on?
- What support do you get from your faith, religious or spiritual identity community?

The spirituality guided visualization exercise (below), which was also covered in Chapter 5, can be offered to clients, to help them connect to their faith, spirituality or belief system, if appropriate.

Tool: Faith, beliefs and spirituality guided visualization exercise

I will walk you through a series of prompts to help you visualize what spirituality means for you.

Open your hands and imagine you are holding spirituality in the palm of your hands like an object.

- What is the shape and size of it?
- What is its weight?
- What is its colour?
- Does it make a sound or is it silent? If a sound, what sound?
- Does it have a scent, smell or fragrance?
- What are you feeling as you hold the object?
- What do you want to do with the object?

Now place the object somewhere safe for you.

- What does this reveal about your relationship with spirituality?
- What role does it play in supporting your counselling? Or in understanding the issues you wish to bring to counselling?

Reflective exercises

Based on your answers to the reflective questions in Chapter 5 on faith, beliefs and spirituality, how might this reflect what you might want to do with your client's faith, spirituality or beliefs? Does it make you want to avoid mentioning or exploring it?

....

....

....

....

....

....

What are the barriers or challenges for you in working with your client's faith or spirituality? Does this mean you can't bring it into the room for your clients?

....

....

....

....

....

....

In thinking of your case study client, how have you worked with their faith, beliefs or spirituality? What may have made it easier to name, explore and work with these?

....

....

....

....

....

....

What might be the barriers or challenges to working with your client's faith, beliefs or spirituality? If faith, beliefs and spirituality haven't come up in the work, why might this be?

....

....

....

....

....

....

Based on the above assessment questions and visualization exercise, how might you now use these in working with your clients? What particularly might be helpful to ask your case study client and why?

....

....

....

....

....

....

Ethnicity and race

For an introduction to the topic of ethnicity and race, see Chapter 6.

Reflective exercises

As we have explored the impact of race and ethnicity on a client's lived experience (Chapters 6–9), why is that impact important to know in counselling?

....

....

....

....

....

....

What might be the impact of a client's ethnicity or racialized identity in counselling and in their therapeutic relationship with you?

....

....

....

....

....

....

With two identities present in the room, both the counsellor's and client's ethnicity and racialized identity are present and having an impact. What will need to be considered is how both the counsellor and client experience and feel working with one another when they are either from similar or different ethnic or racialized identity backgrounds.

Reflective exercises

When working with a client (or thinking about your case study client) from the same ethnicity or racialized identity as you (i.e. you as a culturally close counsellor), consider these questions:

- How do you feel in working with the client?
- What might be the impact on your work together?
- What might be the impact on your therapeutic relationship?
- Does it create any barriers in the work?
- Does it create any barriers to working together relationally?

- What potential prejudice, oppression or collusion might be present?
- What fears or hopes might you have about working with them?

....
....
....
....
....

When working with a client (or thinking about your case study client) from a different ethnicity or racialized identity as you (i.e. you as a culturally distant counsellor), consider these questions:

- How do you feel in working with the client?
- What might be the impact on your work together?
- What might be the impact on your therapeutic relationship?
- Does it create any barriers in the work?
- Does it create any barriers to working together relationally?
- What potential prejudice, oppression or collusion might be present?
- What fears or hopes might you have about working with them?

....
....
....
....

As with culture, faith or any other identity characteristic, our clients are not here for our learning about the wider context or knowledge on these topics. To see the client as our resource to understanding or learning about that identity characteristic is an unethical use of our power in the counselling relationship. Our aim here is to understand our client's relationship with their identity characteristics and how they experience the world and their lived experiences because of their identity and intersectionality.

How your client might feel in working with you is also important to explore with them.

When you and the client first meet and there is a visible racial, ethnic or cultural difference between you, how this is understood, explored and processed (or not) will impact and influence how the therapeutic relationship and process manifests and unfolds, ultimately what happens between the two of you and if the work is felt to have been therapeutic for the client or not.

The client's culture influences and impacts what their expectations are of counselling and how they might show up and relate to you in the therapeutic relationship. We also need to know the influence of race and ethnicity on the issue or presenting problem that the client brings, how these impact on how the problem is spoken about and presented and why, and how these experiences can be explored between counsellor and client. It may be the counsellor's identity that the client is relating to, and this is why they present or do not present their problem and in a particular way.

Below are some prompt questions to help you consider the impact of ethnicity and race in your therapeutic relationships.

Tool: Ethnic and racialized identity questions

- How does the client identify their ethnicity?
- How does the client identify their racialized identity?
- How does the client feel about working with you, as an [insert your ethnic identity] ethnically similar/distant counsellor?
- How does the client feel about working with you, as a [insert your racialized identity – white/Black/Brown] counsellor?
- What might be the impact on your work together?
- What might be the impact on your therapeutic relationship?
- Does it create any barriers in the work?
- Does it create any barriers to working together relationally?
- Has your client chosen to work with you because of any of your identity characteristics? If so, which one, and why?
- What about your other identity characteristics, which were not chosen; do they create any barriers or challenges for the client?
- If your client was allocated to you, how do they feel about working with you, as an [insert your ethnicity/racialized identity]?
- What barriers or impact does your identity create when they have been allocated to you?
- Do you see the client's ethnicity or racialized identity as a cause or solution to their issues or presenting problem?

- Does the client see their ethnicity or racialized identity as a cause or solution to their issues or presenting problem?
- Is your or your client's identity a barrier to the client talking about their issue or presenting problem?
- Does it feel that the client is making assumptions about you, based on your ethnicity or racialized identity? Is this impacting on the relationship or on how the client is talking about their issue?

Reflective exercise

In reading through the identity questions above, note down any thoughts, reflections or questions that may have come up for you. How might you be able to use these identity questions in your therapeutic or supervision practice?

....

....

....

....

....

....

Culturally close and culturally distant identities

There are advantages and disadvantages to being culturally close (perceived identity similarities between counsellor and client) and to being culturally distant (perceived identity differences between counsellor and client).

The advantages of being culturally close include:

- Building the therapeutic relationship quicker and feeling closer, as familiarity promotes a feeling of connection.
- The client is able to engage in the process more easily, through a feeling of familiarity and role-modelling by the counsellor.
- The client feels they are 'being seen'.

- The client feels that they don't need to explain or teach their counsellor about aspects of their identity or lived experiences.
- The client wants a counsellor who is socially located in a similar position to them 'out there' and understands the systemic inequalities experienced.

The disadvantages of being culturally close, which may be the result of cultural misattunement from the counsellor, can include:

- Familiarity leads to the client using the 'you know' response, which fills in the gap instead of explaining, and assumes the counsellor knows and understands the client and so they can stop any further exploration of that point. It can also be used as a defence not to have to explain or explore the client's experience, a defence itself used by either client or counsellor who colludes with the defence and goes along with the 'you know' without exploring it.
- Familiarity also happens the other way around, with the counsellor saying, 'you know', which assumes the client understands them. This is oppressing the client's own experiences and removes the client's ability to say that they don't know, possibly leaving something unsaid and unexplored. The client is being missed and not seen, and the counsellor is not taking time to explore the client's individual lived experiences – this is cultural misattunement.
- Clients worry that confidentiality is compromised because they see the counsellor as being from their same community and so fear that 'news' of their counselling or problems may get back to others within their family or community. This may lead to a break in an honour code and shame if this forms part of their cultural context.
- Familiarity creates unintentional bias, assumptions, or projections onto the client, as the counsellor may be using their own frame of reference or worldview to look at the client's material – again a cultural misattunement.
- The client projects onto the counsellor and assumes what they will get from a counsellor who seems similar or familiar to them – ease of understating or an expectation of understanding, or equally a judgement of the client 'not being good enough' or living up to cultural expectations (a parallel of judgement they may face in their community).
- The client feels conflicted, shame and difficulty if their concern falls outside cultural norms/values, and exploring this causes further shame for the client.
- The client feels distant from their culture and ashamed to share this with a counsellor who is perceived to be close or within that culture.
- The client has higher expectations of what they'll get or special treatment (i.e. reduced fees, crossing boundaries into personal space, counsellor is able to also see other family members as clients).

- Power is not explored and oppression not acknowledged, possibly from a collective collusion of avoiding the topic because they 'are the same' and so there is no power differential.
- The client feels that the counsellor has assimilated to the dominant culture (sold out their culture) to become part of the dominant group to access privileges and power. The client is left feeling abandoned, betrayed or rejected in their identity.
- The counsellor is perceived as delivering a Western (non-culturally close) mode of counselling.
- The client is filled with shame due to them struggling. They believe the counsellor is not and so the counsellor is perceived as having successfully navigated the environment and 'system', unlike the client who may feel like a failure in comparison to the counsellor.
- The counsellor is 'stuck' within their own culture and may feel threatened by the client's rejection of their shared culture.

In being culturally close to your clients, it is important you don't focus solely on the closeness just to highlight and use it to show your understanding of the client. It is also important not to ignore any cultural distance between the two of you. You must hold both closeness and distance in the relationship of your two identities. This reflects being culturally attuned to your clients.

The advantages of being culturally distant include:

- The counsellor has an 'outsider' lens or viewpoint, whereas the client sees it from being on the 'inside'.
- The client doesn't want to work with a counsellor from within their culture as they may want a new perspective which is part of another culture.
- The client doesn't feel judged by someone 'inside' their culture, if the client feels they are distanced from their own culture or doesn't live up to cultural norms or expectations.
- The client requests a culturally distant counsellor to be able to work through issues which were caused because of identity differences and distances.
- Cultural distance is recognized by the counsellor and so the counsellor is intentionally and consciously working on really seeing the client, even if they are anxious about it, and able to address the power differentials between them – this is being culturally attuned.

The disadvantages of being culturally distant, which may be the result of cultural misattunement from the counsellor, can include:

- The 'outsider' lens leads to the counsellor using bias, assumptions or staying in their own frame of reference when relating to and working with the client.
- The client projects onto the counsellor and assumes what they will get from a counsellor who is distanced from them (i.e. lack of understanding).
- The client is with a counsellor who is socially located in a different or opposing position to them 'out there' and may not understand the systemic inequalities experienced.
- Systemic inequalities and power differences are re-enacted in the therapeutic relationship, with the client experiencing further oppression and marginalization from the counsellor.
- Building the relationship is slow, creating distance in the therapeutic relationship, as unfamiliarity promotes a feeling disconnection for the counsellor and/or client.
- The client struggles to engage in the process and/or relationship, through a feeling of unfamiliarity with the counsellor.
- The client feels they are not 'being seen'.
- The client feels that they need to explain or teach their counsellor about aspects of their identity or lived experiences and/or the counsellor asks this of the client, reflecting a counsellor who wants to be 'competent' but not attuned.
- The counsellor wants to 'know' about their client but only wants to learn about the culture itself and not the individual client and their experience of it, with the client feeling invisible and dismissed. Again, this reflects a counsellor who wants to learn cultural 'competence' and not be in cultural attunement with the client.
- The counsellor has anxiety about really 'seeing' their client and feels overwhelmed to 'know' and understand everything about the client's identity characteristics.
- The counsellor is not aware of how much they are 'missing' or not seeing about the client.

In being culturally distant to your clients, it is important you don't expect your clients to act as if they are the teacher to you, teaching you what you can very often find out yourself through research. It is important not to 'miss' the client themselves and their understanding and lived experience of their culture and all aspects of their identity. Don't try to create any 'sameness' to be able to bridge the distance and demonstrate your understanding of the client. You must hold both closeness and distance in the relationship of your two identities.

We need to notice the distances between our own and our client's identity, but we also can't let it dominate whereby we miss the points at which we are culturally close, otherwise we end up relating to each other from a place of distance and difference and fail to consider any cultural closeness and what or how that may impact the relationship. We are most susceptible if the distance comes from a visible external identity characteristic and the culturally close identity comes from an invisible internal identity characteristic. The therapeutic relationship then is being driven by outer differences rather than by inner closeness.

The important question here to ask yourself is whether there is cultural closeness and/or cultural distance. Does it create barriers, challenges or difficulties in your therapeutic relationship? In the process? Does it create further distance between the two of you or does it bring you closer? Does it shut down the work or does it enhance the work?

Reflective exercises

You can ask the same of your case study client: is there cultural closeness and/or cultural distance and where? Does it create barriers, challenges or difficulties in your therapeutic relationship? In the process? Does it create further distance between the two of you or does it bring you closer? Does it shut down the work or does it enhance the work?

....

....

....

....

....

....

In reading through the culturally close and culturally distant advantages and disadvantages above, note down any thoughts, reflections or questions that may have come up for you. How might you be able to use these in understanding your therapeutic relationships?

....

....

....

....

....

....

CHAPTER 14

Component 3: Power

In this chapter, we will explore the presence and impact of power within our therapeutic relationships, what to look for, and how to work within the diversity of power, privilege and oppression. For an introduction to the topic and concept of power, see Chapter 8.

Reflective exercises

Where might there be power and privilege in counselling? (See Chapter 8 for ideas.)

....

....

....

....

....

How might power and privilege show up in the counselling process or therapeutic relationship? How has it or how might it show up in your therapeutic relationship with your case study client? (See Chapter 8 for ideas.)

....

....

....

....

....

....

Intersectional identity and power

For an introduction to the topic and concepts of identity and intersectionality, see Chapter 7.

In any therapeutic relationship there are two identities present, interacting, responding, reacting and relating to one another – the identity of the client and the identity of the counsellor.

The intersectionality of the two identities, which either shifts their power up or down in relation to the other person, impacts on the therapeutic process and relationship. It's important we understand, explore and reflect on our own and our client's intersectionality, so that we can understand the power and privilege held in the identity of the counsellor, the potential power and privilege held in other identity characteristics of the counsellor plus the potential power and privilege held in the client's identity characteristics. We can then explore how this combination might show up as a power differential and power-oppressive relational dynamic in the therapeutic relationship.

By recognizing our own privileged identities, we can own our awareness to not make assumptions about clients, and not automatically or by default view the client through our own worldview lens. It allows us to hold on to the understanding that each of us is socially located in different social contexts and at different places on systems of oppression.

To recognize the oppressive and systemic inequalities 'out there', we can recognize and name them 'in here' and work with and explore how these external contexts impact our clients. We need to be asking and exploring: how are our clients being impacted by systemic and oppressive practice 'out there'? How do I work to be aware of it not repeating 'in here'? So how do I offer something equal and anti-oppressive 'in here'?

Power in the 'in here'

Power and privilege occur within relationships because in relationships the identity of both people is present. And where identity is present, power and privilege (held in the intersectional identities) are present. Therefore, when working relationally, power is always present in counselling and therapeutic relationships. Power, privilege, oppression, identity and intersectionality are part of understanding our client's lived experience 'out there' and in relationships within the external contexts, and so form part of the internal 'in here' context for the therapeutic relationship.

Reflective exercise

Let's explore power 'in here':

1. Where might there be power in counselling?
2. Where might there be power in your identity as a counsellor?
3. Where might there be power in the client (or your case study client) or in their identity?
4. Why might there be power in counselling (or in your case study client's counselling)?
5. What problems do power differences create (in your therapeutic relationship with your case study client)?
6. What examples of power differences are there in therapeutic relationships (or in your therapeutic relationship with your case study client)?

(See Chapter 8 for ideas.)

....

....

....

....

....

....

Power is implicit in any 'helping' role, relationship or dynamic. The action of 'helping' is a power differential, resulting in the power relational dynamic of 'powerful counsellor – less powerful/powerless client'. This power is about the power in the role as counsellor. The client, by their very need for help or support, is vulnerable and potentially powerless, which is then reinforced by positioning the client as powerless in relation to the counsellor.

Helping is a power differential that creates a drama triangle. The drama triangle is all about power and who has power in the relational dynamic (Karpman, 1968), which can be adapted and applied to therapeutic relationships. The counsellor (as helper) is often positioned as the rescuer, as this is the position of the 'powerful responsible' one to help the 'victim' (see Figure 18).

Figure 18: The drama triangle in therapeutic relationships (image adapted from Karpman, 1968)

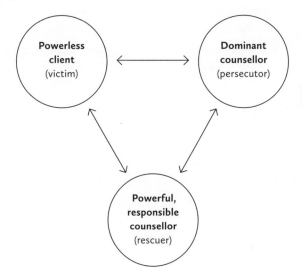

Although the counsellor or client can fall into any one of these three positions, many variables and identity characteristics mean that the counsellor will most likely hold the power position of rescuer. However, that doesn't mean that the counsellor will never fall into the victim or persecutor positions. It is about how the counsellor is both aware of their power and how they are using it. For example, the counsellor becomes powerless (victim) if they feel overwhelmed and shuts down. The counsellor becomes the persecutor (bully/aggressor) if they feel attacked or undermined and so reacts aggressively back to the client (victim). Through intersectional identities, dominant identities can, consciously or unconsciously, seek to oppress, minoritize and 'other' a non-dominant identity client. This drama triangle is a useful framework for understanding if consciously or unconsciously the 'out there' power-oppressive relational dynamics are being played out 'in here'.

There are four types of power (Proctor, 2017) that can be exercised in therapeutic (helping) relationships by counsellors and in supervision relationships by supervisors:

1. Power-over: this is using your power over someone to be able to coerce, dominate, oppress and hold an authority over them. In a therapeutic relationship, this may show up as exercising your authority in your counsellor role; this could be to persuade your client to stay in counselling, to persuade or coerce your client to engage in the therapeutic process in a particular way, to dominate the relationship and process with your own agenda, or to work with the ending in a way that suits you. If your client has a non-dominant intersectional identity, they are even more vulnerable for that power over them to be used in a way that is a repeat of the 'out there' marginalized and oppressed relational experience.

2. Power-from-within: known as personal power, this is power in your own choices and autonomy as well as the power to resist power over you, which leads to an inner resilience and higher level of self-esteem, self-worth and self-value.

3. Power-with: this is the power that resides within relationships between group and community members. The power is in the strength of the group, reflected in the power of connectivity and collaboration. Equality between group members is valued and power-with is only achieved if group members are viewed as equal.

4. Power-to: this is the power of an individual to be successful, from a combination of power-from-within and power-with. This is essentially the power held by a person to achieve because of their own personal power and the power of being supported by a community.

In counselling, we are looking to come from a position of power-from-within, while recognizing that we could use our power from a position of power-over to dominate and oppress our clients, but we resist doing so.

Power in therapeutic relationships

There are three (interconnected) aspects of power present in therapeutic relationships (Proctor, 2017).

1. Role power

This is the power assigned and credited to the counsellor because of their authority and professional status.

The power is also given to the counsellor because they are in the position of being the helper and not the helpee. The counsellor also holds power because of their hierarchical position within a profession, which seeks to support and help the client who needs help. The counsellor holds responsibility and authority over the therapeutic process, which reinforces their status of power. This could lead to a client dismissing their own opinion, knowledge or experience in favour of the counsellor's 'so-called' knowledge and expertise, which is perceived and accepted as 'right' by the client. Within the therapeutic process, it is the counsellor who holds the projected image of being the expert, holding and competently using skills, knowledge and experience. Having expertise and experience in dealing with people's distress reinforces the authority and power in the role.

The danger of role power is its potential level and influence of power over the client (as mentioned in the previous section) and power inequality in the therapeutic relationship. This can include the level of influence the counsellor has over the client, which can look like any attempt to control the process and relationship without the client being able to challenge at all, the client feeling powerless to challenge or disagree with what the counsellor says or being under the influence of the counsellor's view of their narrative or lived experience. This can be felt and described as the counsellor colonizing (taking ownership of) the client's narrative. The counsellor can also exercise their power through controlling the therapeutic frame of starting and ending sessions, establishing the sessions and counselling contract or ending the contract altogether.

The counsellor exercises their power-over not only through what they do but also by what they say. The use of professional language, terminology or jargon, which may be unfamiliar to the client, is a direct reflection of the privilege that the counsellor holds in accessing their professional field and its training and education. If the counsellor is using their professional language, knowing that it is unfamiliar to the client, they are in that moment marginalizing and excluding the client from fully entering the therapeutic process and relationship and engaging in an equal relationship together. Ultimately, if role power is exercised over the client, the client's narrative is invalidated, ignored and dismissed and essentially the client's truth and lived experience are annihilated. This leaves only one truth (the counsellor's) being held as valid in the therapeutic relationship by the counsellor.

It is not a matter of getting rid of the role power, as power is inherent in the role, but rather it is about acknowledging that the role holds power and not exercising that role power over the client.

Reflective exercises

How do you understand your role power? How do your counselling modality and approach deal with your role power?

....

....

....

....

....

....

How has role power shown up in your case study client work or therapeutic relationship? How might you have unintentionally/intentionally used your role power? How have you attempted to flatten your role power in the therapeutic relationship? What might you need to do to flatten your role power?

....

....

....

....

....

....

2. Societal power

This is power given to an individual because of a combination of their identity as a professional, their identity characteristics and intersectional identities and where they are socially located on systems of oppression.

The counsellor, in their power and authority as a professional, and supported by a societal, legal and ethical system, is located within a societal and structural context as holding authority. It is as if the counsellor is backed up and supported by the 'system'.

When the counsellor holds societal power and is there to help and support the client, it reinforces the notion that the client's distress is located and created within the client and not due to their structural position in society.

When distress is located with the individual and doesn't take on board the impact of living in and engaging with systemic inequality and oppressions as the cause of mental distress and ill-health, the responsibility to be 'well' and 'healthy' in the face of systemic inequality and oppression is entirely on the client. It implies that levels of power and powerlessness within people are externally determined and reinforced, yet distress is located with the individual and the responsibility to get better lies with them. Social justice issues and inequalities get ignored and the client is taken out and removed from their external and social contexts. This positions the client in a 'bubble' of individualism, holding their own individual responsibility. Yet the cause of individual distress does not sit with the individual but with the external contexts of systemic inequality. The powerlessness and oppression a client experiences in external contexts reinforces their powerlessness in the position of the client in counselling.

So what does it mean for the client to help themselves, if they are told that they hold responsibility for their distress and are also located on a system of oppression and may be too powerless and oppressed to be able to change if they are of a non-dominant identity? Some clients can make changes and alleviate their distress, because they are located at the dominant end of the power spectrum and can utilize structural power based on their individual intersectional identity. Other clients are unable to make any or as many changes to alleviate their distress, purely because they are located at the non-dominant end of the spectrum without any structural power.

This lack of external context results in and promotes individualism within the counselling process (towards agency, autonomy and change), supporting the societal power and status of counsellors (seen as having agency and autonomy), and holding the client responsible for the degree of change and assuming their level of agency and autonomy to be able to change. If the client is not able to change, they are held responsible and blamed for their individual lack of capability to change, rather than acknowledging the external structures and systems around the client, and this keeps them oppressed, small, marginalized and minoritized.

Rather than colluding with an individual internal power (individualism) we must include and accommodate for the influence and impact of structural and systemic external power on the client's distress, as well as how it is to be alleviated, and the degree of change, agency and autonomy that the client can access because of these external contexts.

Reflective exercises

How do you understand your societal power and what aspects of your identity contribute towards it? How do your counselling modality and approach deal with your societal power? How does your modality view distress in clients? Is there any acknowledgement of the external contexts? How do you or will you work with your societal power in your therapeutic relationships to flatten the power?

....

....

....

....

....

....

How has societal power shown up in your case study client work or therapeutic relationship? How might you have unintentionally/intentionally used your societal power? What level of societal power does your client have? Have you assumed the level of autonomy your client has? How have you viewed their ability and capacity to change? How have you viewed the cause of their distress, as their responsibility? How might you now include and consider the impact of external contexts on the client's distress and on their ability to change?

....

....

....

....

....

....

3. Historical power

This is a person's individual history plus their power held historically resulting in the historical power they hold currently.

A person's relationship history, and how they have experienced, utilized or been subjected to power in those relationships, will determine their relationship blueprint and how that blueprint gets replayed in current relationships. This may lead to many assumptions being made in the therapeutic relationship about the level of power they hold and how to utilize it, as well as the other person's level of power, with an expectation of how the power relational dynamic will play out and unfold between them, based on their own historical power and relationship blueprint.

By recognizing that your own experience of historical power may influence your expectations of how power will be used and related to 'in here', the challenge is to not automatically make assumptions or expectations about the level of power the other person has or how much power you hold and how you will utilize it.

We cannot assume either the level of power or level of oppression that the client experiences, nor can we assume that the therapeutic relationship is automatically an equal one. We need to recognize that both the clients and our own levels of power and experiences of power or powerlessness will be reflected in how each person relates to and manages the power in the therapeutic relationship. What type of power and power dynamic is showing up in the therapeutic relationship? Is it power over the client in a power-oppressive relational dynamic? Or can either one or both hold their own personal power (power-from-within)?

Naming the role power that the counsellor holds supports an open dialogue with the client about how a power relational dynamic may manifest 'in here' in the therapeutic relationship, and creates a gateway to exploring the client's external 'out there' experiences of systemic inequality and systems of oppression.

Reflective exercises

How do you understand your historical power and relationship blueprint and what aspects of your history contribute towards it? How does your historical power influence how you see power being used in your therapeutic relationships? How do you or will you work with your historical power in your therapeutic relationships to flatten the power?

....

....

....

....

....

....

How has historical power shown up in your case study client work or therapeutic relationship? How might you have unintentionally/intentionally used your historical power relationship blueprint? How do you expect your client to use their power? How does your client's historical power show up? What is their historical power relationship blueprint – how do they expect you to use your power, and how do they expect or use their power? In what ways does historical power get used 'in here'?

....

....

....

....

....

....

Power and privilege in the counsellor

Reflective exercises

Where might there be privilege in the counsellor? (See Chapter 8 for ideas.)

....

....

....

....

....

....

Where do you hold power and privilege in your identity and role as the counsellor? (See Chapter 8 for ideas.)

....

....

....

....

....

....

We discussed in the previous section the role power which the counsellor holds and the position of influence, authority and status that it places them in, within the therapeutic relationship. There is the potential for the counsellor to use their power as power over the client or take up the powerful, rescuer position, positioning the client as the 'victim' (in the drama triangle, Figure 18).

Role power is also reflected in the privileges (advantages and benefits) that the counsellor has because of the dominant and powerful role they hold.

Tool: A counsellor's privileges

- Being familiar with and having responsibility and experience to facilitate the counselling.
- Being familiar with and having knowledge and experience of the counselling culture.
- Being familiar with and having knowledge and experience of the counselling process.
- Being familiar with and having knowledge and experience of therapeutic relationships.
- Being familiar with and having knowledge and experience of counselling (as a counsellor or as a counsellor and client).
- Being familiar with and having knowledge and experience of the emergent process.
- Being in control of the counselling and inviting the client into the process and relationship, which you are in control of, facilitating and are familiar with and have knowledge and experience of.

- Having the ability to influence the client.
- Having the ability to comment on the client's narrative, give your perspective or view.
- Being familiar with and having knowledge and experience of how to manage and process the ending.
- Being familiar with and having knowledge and experience of how to conduct assessments and the assessment process.
- Knowing about the client but holding the boundary of self-disclosure and the choice of what to self-disclose.
- Automatically being given credibility in your role, as an effective and helpful professional.
- Being familiar with and having knowledge and experience of professional language.
- Your words and interventions holding weight, value and influence with the client.
- Holding the client's information and narrative, knowing about the client.
- Holding legal, ethical and safeguarding responsibilities, which can include breaking confidentiality with the client and speaking with a third party if necessary.
- Holding the boundaries and therapeutic frame (time, location, fees).
- Being paid by the client.

Reflective exercises

What are your thoughts, reflections and responses to the list of counsellor's privileges? Are some easier or more comfortable to acknowledge and accept as experiencing?

....

....

....

....

....

....

What other privileges can you think of and add to this list?

....

....

....

....

....

....

A counsellor's power and privilege can show up via microaggressions aimed at the client because of the power-oppression relational dynamic being replayed. (For more information on microaggressions, see Chapter 9.)

Microaggression can show up in counselling or the therapeutic relationship, for example as:

- the counsellor feeling negative towards the client (due to the client's identity) so the counsellor may refuse or avoid working with the client or with a particular client group because of their shared identity characteristic, which the counsellor is uncomfortable with or biased, prejudiced, rejecting or devaluing of, which can lead to marginalizing and excluding the client from accessing counselling
- the counsellor, while in therapeutic relationship with the client, routinely dismissing, oppressing, insulting, disrespecting or invalidating the client
- the counsellor, feeling challenged to hold 'two truths', invalidating, minimizing, dismissing or reinterpreting the client's narrative or lived experience to fit with their own worldview.

Power and privilege in identity of person as counsellor

While the counsellor holds power and privilege through their role power as a counsellor, they can also hold additional power and privilege in their intersectional identities. (For more information about intersectional identities, see Chapter 7.)

Applicable to therapeutic relationships, we need to know what our intersectional identities are, as many factors of our identity mean we move up and down that spectrum of power-oppression accordingly and this will impact on how the client perceives and relates to us. Our ethnicity, gender, age, ability/disability and other visible identity characteristics hold greater weight to how much we move up or down that spectrum.

These are important factors to consider when in a therapeutic relationship and welcoming in clients with their diversity and range of intersectional identities. In the therapeutic relationship itself, the two identities are both influential in the impact of the work and how the relationship itself and the process unfold and are experienced.

Identity characteristics which shift power up include professional status as a counsellor, being racialized as white, being from an upper or middle-class background and being English-speaking, as these are dominant identity groups and will raise power and privilege in therapeutic relationships. What else would you add?

Identity characteristics which shift power down include being ethnically minoritized, being racialized as Black or Brown, being from a working-class background and English-speaking but not as a first language, as these are non-dominant identity groups that will lower power and privilege in therapeutic relationships, while holding and maintaining power through role power as a counsellor. If you were not the counsellor, but the client with this intersectional identity, it would 'complement' and further shift your power down.

Figure 19: Scales of Power in Identity Characteristics in Counselling

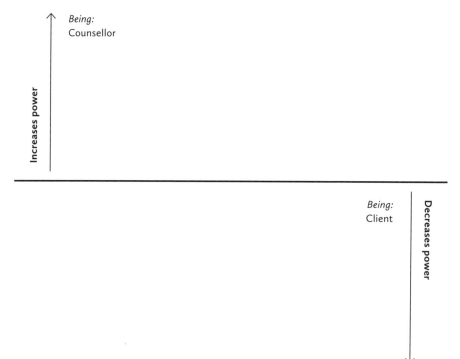

168

Activity: Which of your identity characteristics would you add to either arrow (see Figure 19)? A template of the Scales of Power in Identity Characteristics in Counselling tool is also included in the online Appendix.

Reflective exercises

What aspects of your identity increase or decrease your power and status?

....

....

....

....

....

....

If you are from a dominant identity group, what position of dominance or privileges might you be consciously or unconsciously holding? How might that show up in the work? How has this shown up in your work and relationship with your case study client?

....

....

....

....

....

....

If you are from a non-dominant identity group, what position of oppression or disadvantage might you be consciously or unconsciously holding? How might that show up in the work? How has this shown up in your work and relationship with your case study client?

....

....

....

....

....

....

What influence or impact do you think your perceived identity by clients has on your work and therapeutic relationships? How has this shown up in your work and relationship with your case study client?

....

....

....

....

....

....

Our identity is not only disclosed through visible identity characteristics, but we also self-disclose through our communication style, through our dress, through our body language and through any visible symbols, signs or identifiers of an aspect of our internal (invisible) identity characteristic. What is being disclosed will influence your relationship and potentially exert power over the client.

Reflective exercise

What might your dress sense, appearance, accent or any other identifiers of your internal identity disclose about you to your client? What impact or influence does this have on your clients and relationship? How does this impact the power relational dynamic? What position are you placing yourself in? What position are you placing the client in, in relation to you? How has this shown up in your work and relationship with your case study client?

....

....

....

....

....

....

Credibility

Our perceived identity as the counsellor by the client will influence how they relate to us and engage in the process, and this is true of the level and type of credibility the client gives us. There are two types of credibility: ascribed credibility and achieved credibility. The type and level of credibility the client assigns to you is based on your perceived intersectional identity.

Ascribed credibility refers to the credibility automatically given to you because of your identity characteristics signalling either a dominant social or cultural value, which the other person sees as a positive value to have. Ascribed credibility is a form of professional privilege. For example, white-racialized men (two dominant social identities) are automatically ascribed credibility (status, recognition, competency) in their job because of the status, power and privilege given to their dominant identity characteristics. A counsellor is automatically assigned ascribed credibility (status, recognition and competency) in their job because the role is valued by the client. The client automatically believes that a person in the role of counsellor is credible. The job title brings its own privilege via the credibility it is ascribed. In counselling itself, ascribed credibility can support a client to build a rapport and trusting therapeutic relationship quicker if they believe that the counsellor is credible in their job (Eleftheriadou, 1994).

Achieved credibility refers to credibility attained through achievements. This can include the more traditional achievements through qualifications, promotions and awards. Achieved credibility can also be awarded through the perceived competence of skills, experience and knowledge, demonstrated in the process and therapeutic relationship, as perceived by the client. Our achieved credibility gets raised or lowered based on the client's assessment of our competence of skills, experience and knowledge (i.e. how good a job we are perceived to be doing).

Privilege is through ascribed credibility (instead of achieved credibility). Privilege is not needing to prove your expertise, skills, knowledge or experience. You have ascribed credibility based on your identity, whereas some of us must prove ourselves through attained credibility via qualifications, awards and status.

Reflective exercises

Are you assigned ascribed credibility or achieved credibility? What aspects of your identity reflect achieved credibility and ascribed credibility?

....

....

....

....

....

....

Have you felt the need to achieve (work for and prove) your credibility? If so, which aspect of your intersectional identity is that due to?

....

....

....

....

....

....

What influence or impact do you think your ascribed or achieved credibility has on your work and therapeutic relationships?

....

....

....

....

....

....

How does your case study client assign you ascribed or achieved credibility? What aspects of your identity is this based on? What impact does your credibility have on the work and relationship? Did you need to demonstrate your credibility to your client? And if so, why?

....

....

....

....

....

....

Power and privilege in identity of person as client

When a counsellor holds multiple identities of minoritization, the therapeutic relationship can be challenged through a power-oppression dynamic. The client, in identifying a minoritized identity characteristic in the counsellor, for which the client holds a dominant identity in relation to it, may support a power relational dynamic in which the client moves into the dominant position and relocates the counsellor to a marginalized position in relation to them.

Instead of the counsellor using power over the client, the client uses their power (from a dominant identity characteristic) for power over the counsellor, to see them as inferior, 'less than' and 'not good enough' because of the counsellor's non-dominant identity. The client devalues, dismisses, rejects, avoids or minimizes the counselling process, the counselling space or the therapeutic relationship. It could be communicated through the client feeling that the counsellor may be lacking in some way – in understanding of them, in professional experience, in life experience, in relatability, in cultural closeness or in credibility (see previous section on credibility).

Reflective exercises

Thinking of your case study client, what does the Identity Wheel reveal about their social location, place on the power-oppression spectrum, their intersectionality and intersectional identities?

....

....

....

....

....

....

Where might there be privilege in the identity of the client? Where might the client hold a dominant identity over you? How might the client want to use their power over you?

....

....

....

....

....

....

How might or does their privilege show up in your relationship? How do you experience being oppressed by your client?

....

....

....

....

....

Two intersectional identities in therapeutic relationship

In exploring the intersectionality, power, privilege and oppression in the identity of both the counsellor and the client, when we look at both in relationship, it supports us to understand which privileged and marginalized identities are present in the room and therapeutic relationship. It is important to stress that within these two intersectional identities, both privileged and oppressed identity characteristics can be present in the counsellor and in the client. In exploring your and your client's intersectional identity, it is important to identify the privileged and oppressed identities, without colluding to prioritize or highlight oppressed and disadvantaged identity characteristics, or leaving privileged identity characteristics unnamed, pushed into the background, hidden or invisible.

Activity: Using the Scales of Relational Power tool below (Figure 20), identify and fill in the arrows with which privileged and oppressed identity characteristics you and your client hold. You can think of your case study client for this exercise. A template of this tool is also included in the online Appendix.

Figure 20: Scales of Relational Power tool (template)

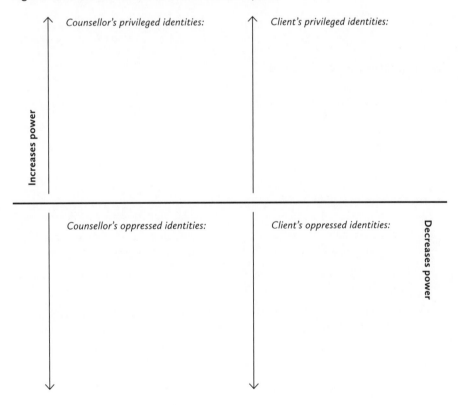

175

Reflective exercise

Having filled this out, what does it reveal to you about the two intersectional identities? Does one hold more power and privilege than the other? How might power-over be used to marginalize the non-dominant identity of the other person? Who is using their power-over? What impact might this have on your therapeutic process and relationship? What do you now need to consider or take notice of in working with your client, or with any client?

....

....

....

....

....

....

Rebalancing power 'in here'

We need to promote and support the therapeutic process, relationship and space to offer anti-oppressive practice, whereby the power is equalized and flattened between counsellor and client. We need a hierarchy-free and privilege-free process and relationships to support the power-from-within, power-with and power-to for our clients.

To address and rebalance power we need to:

- recognize that the client is responsible, capable, has agency (autonomy) and is in need of help at the same time, which are not mutually exclusive to one another
- focus on the client and being alongside them (as if a passenger in the car) rather than in the power-over position of expert
- create a positive, supportive therapeutic relationship and working alliance, in which the client can build trust with the counsellor and process, and view the work as credible, and themselves as able to do the work
- be aware of the language we use as the counsellor and avoid using jargon
- be aware of language used by client, and, if there is language of 'oppression'

in the client's narrative (i.e. powerlessness, struggle, discrimination), explore their experiences of relational oppression 'out there' and bring those external contexts more explicitly into the work 'in here'

- work with and explore the client's external context experiences of systemic inequality and oppression. The Power Threat Meaning Framework (Johnstone & Boyle, 2018) offers us exploratory questions (see Figure 14), which we can ask our client to help us identify their experiences and relationship with power
- examine the therapeutic process and relational dynamic for signs of power and oppression being re-enacted from either the counsellor or client.

Reflective exercise

Reflecting on your case study client, how might you rebalance the power differential in your therapeutic relationship? What aspect of power, privilege or oppression might you need to pay particular attention to?

....

....

....

....

....

....

CHAPTER 15

Component 4: Therapeutic Relationship

In this chapter, we will explore the therapeutic relationship and how to build, work with and understand the relationship, while identifying what to consider about the relationship when working within the diversity of structural contexts, identity and power.

Safe spaces

For an introduction to the topic of safe spaces and belonging, see Chapter 11.

In that earlier chapter, you were invited to complete a 'Street Map' exercise and explore what it revealed about your identity, your intersectionality and your lived experience. I invited you to think about whether you experienced the 'out there' space as safe or unsafe and if you felt you belonged in those spaces or not. In reflecting on how you experience spaces 'out there', let's move our focus to how you and your clients may experience spaces in counselling.

Reflective exercises

As the counsellor, does the 'in here' space feel safe to you, and do you feel that you belong in it?

....

....

....

....

....

....

How and why does 'in here' feel safe or unsafe to you? Why do you feel that you belong or don't belong in it?

....

....

....

....

....

....

How might your experience of 'in here' help you to understand if your client feels safe 'in here'? What might your client need from you and from the 'in here' space to feel safe and that they belong 'in here'?

....

....

....

....

....

....

If the 'out there' space feels unsafe for clients then by default it is highly likely that the 'in here' space will also feel unsafe for clients, because it is contained within the 'out there' space. If the world 'out there' is untrustworthy, then 'in here' is also untrustworthy.

The counsellor needs to create trust with the client for the client to feel safe 'in here' and with the counsellor. As counsellors, we have responsibility to create safe spaces for clients, but it is entirely up to the client if it feels safe for them. If it doesn't feel safe for the client, we need to be humble and culturally attuned to understand why this is and what we need or can do to support them to feel safe. We cannot make the client feel safe. We cannot assume or expect the client to feel safe. We may not be able to create a safe space for the client to feel safe. It is not a definite or given that a client will feel safe. Especially if there are power differentials, the client may feel dismissed, not seen, as if they won't be understood, that they can't trust the counsellor and therefore feel unsafe. The space 'in here' is relational, it's evolving and fluid, it needs tending to; it is not something that gets created at the start and forgotten about, pushed into the background. It is not a given that if it is built as safe it will remain safe. It needs tending to because it is part of the relationship between you and your client.

We need to take responsibility for what we can do in sessions to create safety, not just for the space itself but how we show up relationally and the process we are facilitating. For there to be a safe space, the needs of the client must be met in the space and through the therapeutic relationship and it must be a space where the process of exploration can happen and the client can engage in it.

We are creating a space that the client feels they can step into. Therefore, does it feel like a safe space? A client can enter the space, but this doesn't automatically mean that it feels safe for them. Don't assume that consent to entering the space indicates they are feeling safe in it. The 'safety questions' tool (below) offers a range of questions to help you explore how the space is being created, what is needed in the space for it to be safe for the client and how we are relating to and utilizing the space, which potentially can lead to the client feeling unsafe in the space and relationship. These questions are a tool which you can use in your process reflections, as well as adapting them as part of your assessment process and dialogue with clients in building your working alliance and therapeutic relationship. Of course, these questions can also be used to monitor the ongoing therapeutic space and relationship, to ensure that safety is being maintained and that the space is being reviewed, so as counsellors we don't get complacent about the space and its safety for clients, which could be experienced as an oppressive and power-over behaviour by counsellors against the clients.

Tool: Safety questions

- Without safety, what are the consequences?
- To create a safe space and make the space feel safe for the client, what does the client need from me?
- What does the client need from themselves?

- What needs are to be seen and met in the client?
- What aspects of my identity need to be met and acknowledged?
- Does the space become a space for the client to step into and bring themselves?
- Has the space been filled up or does it feel full up?
- How do we fill up the space intentionally/unintentionally? How are we oppressing the client by not having the space to feel safe in or to feel they can speak?
- Am I doing all the talking? Am I interrupting or dominating the conversation?
- Am I not holding silences or breaking silences?
- Am I creating my own agenda, leading the client, choosing what to focus on, not giving the client autonomy to use the space in the way they need to?
- Am I pushing the client too quickly or too deeply? Am I skimming over their material? Am I not staying with feelings? Am I not working at depth? Am I dismissing narrative or feelings or experiences? What am I doing with the client's content (narrative, feelings, experiences)?
- Have I created a space for the client to step into?
- Am I introducing a topic for discussion and asking the client into that space to think about it? When I see they are uncomfortable with the topic, but I am not, am I forcing that on to the client oppressively?
- What might be the client's experiences of entering spaces 'out there'?
- Have they experienced safe spaces? What has been their past experiences of safe spaces? Are they familiar or comfortable with safe spaces?
- How might their 'out there' or past experiences of safe spaces get repeated 'in here'? How might the client relate to me 'in here'? What might the client expect from me 'in here'?

There is a link between belonging and safe spaces. Being in a space doesn't automatically make you feel safe and therefore you don't automatically feel that you belong in that space, are welcomed there, seen as an equal or that you are being included. How do we create safety, if we don't know what safety means to our clients or what helps them to feel safe? How will we know what the elements are that make up the client feeling safe 'in here' with us? The 'belonging questions' tool (below) offers several questions to help you explore and reflect on how and if the client feels they belong in the space 'in here'.

Tool: Belonging questions

- Does the client feel a sense of belonging to the space? To the therapeutic relationship?
- Does this depend on the identity of the counsellor?
- Does the client want to be matched with a culturally close or culturally distant counsellor to feel a sense of safety and belonging?
- If the client feels safe and has a sense of belonging 'in here', how does that relate to and reveal their history of where they have felt safe and had a sense of belonging 'out there' or in their past?

Reflective exercise

In exploring your experiences of safe space, what relevance, impact or insight does this give you in your work with clients? What has made a space feel safe for you? What was present or absent? How do you know you feel safe and/or have a sense of belonging in a space?

....

....

....

....

....

....

For a client, feeling safe is a fundamental factor in what might make them start, access or leave counselling. Their sense of containment in counselling and their experience of a space which feels accepting, non-judgemental and where they can bring all parts of their identity and lived experience play a big part in supporting the client to feel safe.

Using your client case study, what has been your experience of creating a safe space for them? How have you supported your client to feel safe? Or has that been difficult? If so, why? Why might the client be feeling unsafe in the space and/or relationship? How might their experience of feeling safe or unsafe be linked to your two identities? Does the client feel they belong in the space with you and why? What is present or absent for the client to feel that they either belong or don't belong in the space?

....

....

....

....

....

....

....

....

....

....

Barriers to counselling

Identity and particularly the identity characteristics of culture, ethnicity and faith can create many barriers to counselling. They can include:

- A culture where mental health and mental health issues are not spoken about.
- A family or community culture where they keep issues within the family, don't take issues seriously and feel they can deal with it within the family, leaving a person possibly feeling isolated and unable to access help.
- A cultural honour code where seeking help from the outside is taboo and there is a fear that it may affect the family's reputation and result in shame on the person and family.
- A cultural-based shame or embarrassment of family or the community in

finding out the person did access help or support outside the family or community (possibly an honour code itself being broken).

- In a collectivist 'we' culture, the fear of lack of privacy and confidentiality and the fear of the family or community finding out, which could be from a fear of being seen to enter or exit the counselling building. This may lead to the client being stopped from attending sessions and forced to end the therapy.
- In the collectivist 'we' culture, the fear of doing something without permission and without the authority of elders or parents, which is in line with their lack of choice and autonomy.
- A cultural belief in not recognizing a concern as a mental health issue. What might be defined as 'mental health' in one country may not be so in another; for example, hearing voices in some cultures is seen as being blessed and you are revered for it.
- A cultural belief that any mental health struggle or difficulty is a sign of lack of faith or weak faith and reflects the religiosity of a person.
- A cultural belief that the expression of distress is through the body rather than as psychological distress (somatization), and it is socially and culturally accepted to express physical distress and have it treated medically.
- The cultural differences between emotional expressiveness; in some cultures to express emotions is acceptable, whereas other cultures are not so open to expressing certain feelings.
- The cultural stigma and taboo of mental health.
- Feeling judged by attending counselling and/or by the counsellor.
- The fear of treatment and what to expect in counselling, so a person stays away and doesn't access support.
- The ethical and racial fear of racism or discrimination.

Reflective exercises

Have you experienced any of these barriers yourself? What are your thoughts and reflections about the barriers clients face?

....

....

....

....

....

....

....

....

Thinking of your case study client, what might be the barriers they experience in accessing therapy with you? What barriers might they be jumping over to attend sessions with you?

....

....

....

....

....

....

....

Impact on the therapeutic relationship

As mentioned, the starting point is to acknowledge that both your identity and the client's identity are fully present in the room (the 'two identities' principle). You need to create safety while acknowledging where and why there might be barriers, why the client may find it difficult to trust you or feel safe, and what stops them from bringing their full self and real lived experiences into the room and relationship with you.

What can support the client to engage in counselling is to build a therapeutic relationship that is invitational for the client to enter the relationship, while also being educational about counselling. An explanation and exploration of what the counselling process is can often alleviate a client's fears of what they will be 'doing' 'in here', especially if they are new to counselling and don't know what to expect from the process or relationship.

Working relationally means the counsellor 'sits beside' the client and not 'over' them from a position of expert, power, analysis, interpretation and meaning-making for the client. Instead we are facilitating a process for the client to explore and come to an understanding of their own experiences, for them to find the meaning and allow for meaning-making to happen.

We need to be understanding of our identity and how it relates to the client's, and recognize what power differentials there may be. How might the client be experiencing you? How might they be experiencing the process? Is it something familiar to them or not? Does it create feelings of unsafety because it's unfamiliar?

We need to explore the client's feelings towards being in a therapeutic relationship with a culturally, ethnically, racially or faith-distant counsellor. We need to be able to engage and be open to facilitating, exploring and hearing from the client how they feel towards us as the counsellor. Can we bear to sit with the expectations and assumptions clients are making about us and the work we are offering them to engage in with us?

This will help to build the trust in the relationship as well as the understanding of two identities, two truths and two lived experiences 'in here' and that it is two 'full' people in the room, in relationship with one another. We can't 'park' to one side any aspect of our identity; it all has meaning, impact and influence on what is happening 'in here', in the relationship and in the process.

Ultimately are we helping our clients to show up as their true, authentic selves and support the building of a therapeutic relationship with our authentic self? And do we have the courage to acknowledge all that comes with two diverse identities in relationship with one another? Are we facilitating a process in which the client can safely engage, and allowing for the emergence of understanding through the process and therapeutic relationship itself?

Clients in therapeutic relationship

Clients may come to counselling with an idea, projection or assumption of the perceived identity of the counsellor and of the counselling relationship.

The role of counsellor is often culturally based, as discussed in Chapter 13, and so the therapeutic relationship is often approached through the client's cultural identity and lens of engaging in relationships 'out there'.

Collectivist-identity clients in relationship with culturally close counsellors may ask personal questions, such as asking the counsellor about their relationship and family status or about the counsellor's ethnicity or heritage. When we think of collectivist clients understanding their own self or identity as a 'we', in asking personal questions, the client is trying to identify you as a 'we', how you are linked and related to your family and community, how you are socially located within your identity and are part of a collectivist community. These questions are a way of clients being able to locate you in the relational and collectivist structure of their identity, working out how they add you into their 'we' structure and network of people and relationships.

Culturally distant, non-dominant and marginalized clients, in therapeutic relationship with a dominant identity counsellor, will bring into the therapeutic relationships (consciously or unconsciously) their lifetime of prejudices, oppression, marginalization and minoritization experiences, based on the power differential 'in here' in the therapeutic relationship mirroring their 'out there' lived experiences of power differential relationships. Why would the client expect anything different 'in here' when they start counselling and building a relationship?

The client's expectations, assumptions or projections may include:

- Not feeling safe or not feeling they belong in the counselling relationship, process or space.
- Feeling anger, shame or distrust because they don't feel safe or as if they belong 'in here'.
- The counsellor dismissing, devaluing or minimizing the client's lived experiences or feelings, especially of experiences of racism, prejudice, stereotyping and oppression.
- The counsellor denying the client's experiences or feelings in a way that suppresses the client, and disbelieving their narrative: 'It couldn't have happened like that; it couldn't have been that bad'. This is a form of gaslighting the client.
- Seeing the counsellor as belonging to the dominant identity group and therefore part of the systemic and structural problem, as well as positioning the counsellor as someone who holds the same prejudiced or biased views.
- Holding the counsellor in a superior position, placing them on a pedestal or seeing them as the expert or authority figure 'in here'.
- Seeing the counsellor in this superior position and therefore taking on board the counsellor's worldview or lens of how they see, understand and make sense of their own experience, and disregarding their own feelings, meaning, understanding or lens of how they originally saw it for themselves.
- Feeling inferior, powerless and unable to stand up to the counsellor. This could include not being able to disagree with the counsellor, not being able to make requests, such as changing the day or time of the session, or not being able to end the counselling and struggling to vocalize this.
- Feeling powerless to end the counselling prematurely and waiting for either the counsellor to end it or the counselling contract to come to an end. In a premature ending, the client can feel rejected or abandoned, which could

repeat their 'out there' experiences in relationships or may reflect their experiences of ending relationships with those who are from the dominant identity group.

Reflective exercises

Thinking of your case study client, how might you understand how the client experiences the process and relationship? How might the client be experiencing you in the therapeutic relationship? What expectations and assumptions does the client have about you? What are these based on? Are they based on any aspect of your identity?

....

....

....

....

....

....

....

How have you experienced the therapeutic relationship? How have you experienced working relationally with the client? How might this be influenced by your two identities in relationship with each other?

....

....

....

....

....

....

....

How did you experience the ending or how might you experience the ending with the client? How have you been challenged by the client in your boundaries or therapeutic frame? How did you deal with it?

....

....

....

....

....

....

What we can do to help build the therapeutic relationship and engage in an effective process:

- Recognize the relationship of two people (the intersectionality and identity of two people) and its impact on the therapeutic relationship, as we've discussed already and in the other chapters.
- Be a learner and apply cultural attunement. Always be curious about your client and invite them to tell you more about their lived experiences and their relationship with all the parts of their identity.
- Monitor both of your communication styles. Clients may not open and divulge family problems, which may be due to culture, honour codes and shame, or feeling unsafe or as if they do not belong 'in here'. They may not respond openly to direct questions. They may be reluctant to express negative or what they perceive to be bad or negative thoughts and feelings (as a reflection of their 'we' culture and loyalty to their family). Therefore, it is important that we do not interpret lack of direct disclosure or feelings as resistance or defensiveness. We need to take the time with clients to build up a safe space, where the client feels safe and that they belong in it.
- Don't rush at the beginning. When doing an assessment, take your time to build up trust first before asking questions about what may seem like a sensitive topic for your client, especially as it may be a topic or behaviour that conflicts with their culture, heritage or faith, such as drinking alcohol or sexual or intimate relations, or a shame-based topic such as abuse. Questions asked too quickly may directly affect the client's loyalty or duty to family honour and personal shame. They may feel they are betraying

their family in disclosing this. Enquire gently, be patient, do not expect or demand answers.

Reflective exercise

Thinking of your case study client, what might you now do differently or keep the same, to build a therapeutic relationship with them? What are you now aware of in your therapeutic relationship, or an aspect of it that was impacting or influencing your relationship that you were not aware of before?

....

....

....

....

....

....

CHAPTER 16

Component 5: Therapeutic Process

In this chapter, we will explore the therapeutic process, how it unfolds and what we need to consider when working within the diversity of structural contexts, identity, power and relationship.

Emergent and directive processes

Activity: In thinking about emergent and directive processes, before we start, I would like to invite you to take part in a process exercise. In the box below I would like you to draw a container. I've provided an example of a drawing of a container (see Figure 21).

Figure 21: Container example

Now in your container I would like you to draw a big scribble. Here's an example of mine below (see Figure 22)!

Figure 22: Big scribble exercise

That scribble is known as an emergent process – a process that unfolds and emerges in time, live, and as you are doing it. There is not a set route or predetermined end point. We arrive at the end point because of the emergent process and the end point emerges as we continue the process. We tend to use an emergent process in counselling, as this type of process is all about the experience of doing it (talking) and what emerges from doing it (insight, awareness) for the client. It is not about what it looks like.

Some modalities may use a directive process, in which the outcome, route and process is known. There is a set route and predetermined end point to reach. In an emergent process, the outcome, route and end point are unknown to you and the client. It is important to recognize the difference between emergent and directive processes.

Dependent on the counselling modality, the process can either be emergent or directive, but is most often an emergent one. Talking therapy (as an emergent process) is a Western cultural norm. The emergent process and directive process are cultural elements of counselling. If we see the emergent process as a form of play, which is cultural in its content, then experiencing play as an emergent process may not be familiar to everyone, as play as an emergent process may not be part of everyone's culture, upbringing or lived experience. Some clients may not be used to playing at all. The play 'switch' inside them either never got turned on or was quickly switched off because culturally play was not prioritized. This may be due to lots of reasons, including the culture instead prioritizing or focusing on education, seeing play as a waste of time or being in a family, community or cultural context where they were 'surviving' and couldn't 'indulge' in play. They didn't have the 'luxury' for play, parents were working all hours and there was limited access to resources. This may reflect a non-dominant, minoritized community without access to the privilege of play.

So in counselling, for clients who are unfamiliar with an emergent process, talking therapy can become a vast, unsafe, overwhelming and unknown experience or expectation for them. This can show up as being unable to be spontaneous or in the moment they may freeze, be unable to participate, or feel unsure of what to do.

However, there may be clients who have experienced play but only as a directive and end product or outcome-orientated process. In counselling, this will show up in how the client approaches talking therapy with the same expectation of the process being directive, such as identifying the known end point and the process of how to get there and looking to the counsellor to guide them easily and effectively to that end point and outcome.

Reflective exercises

Take a moment to reflect on the 'big scribble' exercise, how did it feel for you to engage in an emergent process activity? Did it feel safe for you to do it? Were you hesitant or anxious about how it might turn out, look like or if you had 'done it right'?

....

....

....

....

....

....

....

If you asked your case study client to do this activity, how might they engage in it? Might it feel safe or unsafe to not know the outcome or not be directed in how the scribble was to be scribbled or what it needed to look like at the end?

....

....

....

....

....

....

....

An emergent process might create barriers to the work, but rather than it being interpreted as a defence against the presenting problem or issue itself, it could be seen as a defence against how the client feels 'in here'.

Reflective exercises

What is your experience of play growing up? How do you feel when asked to engage in an emergent process or activity? Do you experience any resistance to engaging in the process?

....

....

....

....

....

....

....

....

How might clients feel if they have not experienced emergent play? What barriers might an emergent (unknown) process create for clients?

....

....

....

....

....

....

Using your case study client, how have they experienced the counselling emergent process 'in here' with you?

....

....

....

....

....

....

Counselling culture

Counselling has its own culture, built from values, ethics, beliefs, expectations of behaviour and engagement in the process and a worldview lens of how it relates to, engages with and sees the world. This is reflected through the different modality practices, the therapeutic relationships and the set-up, creation and facilitation of the counselling process.

As with any culture, those who are familiar with it understand its embedded approach of how to engage in that cultural process. When the process is situated within a counselling culture, there needs to be an understanding that not all clients will be aware or familiar with the culture or process, and some education may need to be offered to them about what counselling is at the initial or assessment stages. Often an explanation of your approach plus the need for the client to experience it in action is required.

Reflective exercise

What is your counselling culture? What are the cultural rules, beliefs, expectations and systems in your clinical practice? Would it be familiar or applicable across all cultures? Does it take cultural differences into consideration? If so, how? If not, how/ what does it not take into consideration?

....

....

....

....

....

....

Tool: Counselling culture questions for counsellor to consider

- Can any of the process or culture be explained beforehand in your contract, assessment or first session? If so, what will need to be explained?
- How familiar is the client with your counselling culture and process?
- How does the client's level of familiarity or lack of familiarity impact on them being able to access and engage in the process? How might it show up in the work, in the process, in their level of engagement and in the therapeutic relationship?
- What impact will this have on the therapeutic relationship? How might a client's lack of familiarity reflect a power differential relational dynamic between the counsellor and client?
- The emergent or directive process of counselling may be more widely accessible to dominant or privileged identities and may feel inaccessible or unsafe for non-dominant minoritized identities. How might a client's lack of familiarity be a repeated experience of the client feeling marginalized, minoritized or on the outside or unable to access a service?

- If there is a lack of familiarity, what barriers does this create for the client? How easy is it for the client to jump those barriers?
- If there is a lack of familiarity, what fears or anxieties may this create for the client? How might you alleviate those fears or anxieties?

The 'counselling culture questions' tool (above) lists a range of questions to support you to consider and understand how your clients may be experiencing the counselling process and its emergent process and their relationship to the emergent process. These questions can be used in your reflections about your clients or can be thought about as you undertake your assessment or initial sessions with the client, to help you identify how they relate to the emergent process.

If your counselling approach, modality or practice is an emergent or directive process, does this get explained to your client? This can often support the client to avoid being a compliant or 'good client' or questioning if they are doing the right thing or have the right answer. It can also stop them feeling anxious about what is expected of them 'in here'.

Reflective exercises

What assumptions or expectations are you making of your clients? What might you be assuming about their readiness to engage in the emergent or directive process? Or their experience or familiarity of engaging in the process of play? What about their experience or ability to be spontaneous in the emergent process? Or their experience of feeling safe to play in the emergent process and be spontaneous?

....

....

....

....

....

....

....

....

What have you now realized that is part of your counselling culture that you were not aware of previously? What assumptions have you made about your counselling modality? Or about your client's knowledge and understanding of counselling and the counselling process/relationship?

....

....

....

....

....

....

What aspects of the counselling culture and process do you now need to add into your assessment process, contract or first session? What does the client need to explicitly know about the counselling culture that will make it easier for them to engage in the process and not feel marginalized or oppressed?

....

....

....

....

....

....

Key aspects of the counselling culture may include the following, which are adaptable for each therapeutic modality and their own counselling culture:

- Focusing on change in the client through a therapeutic process.
- Engaging in a therapeutic relationship.
- Attending regular (usually weekly) sessions.
- Committing to a time-specified (short-term or long-term) process.
- Signing a counselling contract.

- Working within the therapeutic frame, which may feel more rigid in its set day, time and fee for sessions.
- Identifying therapeutic goals.
- Valuing insight, self-awareness and personal growth.
- Engaging in an emergent or directive process, dependent on the therapeutic modality.
- Creating a space for meaning-making through a process instead of being given advice, solutions or 'quick fixes'.

Reflective exercises

How might you further refine these aspects to define and explain your counselling modality and culture?

....

....

....

....

....

....

Thinking of your case study client, in what ways were they unfamiliar with the counselling culture and process? What aspects of the counselling culture did you need to explain to your client? What aspects were they familiar/unfamiliar with? Did any of the counselling cultural aspects that you needed to explain or found that the client already knew surprise you?

....

....

....

....

....

....

Identifying as the client, what would have been or what would be helpful to have explained to you about the counselling culture? If you are of a dominant majority or non-dominant marginalized identity, how might your identity impact on your ability to engage in the process or be familiar with the process? What would you need to have in place or explained to you to feel safe and that you understood what was expected of you in the process? How might you apply this to your practice, for your dominant and non-dominant identity clients?

....

....

....

....

....

....

....

....

Impacts on the therapeutic process

A client's identity, intersectionality and lived experiences will have an impact and influence over their engagement, expectations and assumptions across a range of factors that are part of the counselling process. I explore each factor in the process, in turn below, with prompt questions to help you reflect on how these may show up in your therapeutic process and relationships.

Therapeutic culture

Setting up and explaining the therapeutic culture helps to acclimatize clients to an unfamiliar culture and process. If the client is not culturally acclimatized, they may leave or end the counselling quickly or abruptly.

The cultural elements of the therapeutic relationship, and its boundaries, alongside the boundaries, timings, setting, therapeutic frame, context and location of counselling, may be unfamiliar to the client. These need to be made explicit for the client, so that you can offer an anti-oppressive working alliance and therapeutic relationship that focuses on the shared meaning and understanding of the counselling culture.

Role of counselling

Clients will be bringing their own expectations, assumptions and beliefs about the counselling process, the counsellor's role and responsibilities, and their goals or expected outcomes from counselling into the work from the start. The purpose of the work being done 'in here', the setting of an agenda, how you work and all elements of the contract (time, frequency of sessions, location, fee payments) need to be made explicit to clients at the very start.

Therapeutic goals

Therapeutic goals, as part of the counselling process, are a cultural aspect and may be unfamiliar to clients. Even if the goals themselves are identified at the start, the route to achieving them may be via the emergent process of reflection, insight and gaining self-awareness or via the directive process of solution-focused or cognitive techniques. The client may assume that the process to achieve their goals is via a directive process or that they don't want to work on any internal change but are focused on the external applicable solutions. Both the goals and the process of achieving their goals need to be explored in the early stage of enquiry, assessment and the first session.

The process of identifying the goals themselves also needs to be considered. The client may want to focus on one presenting problem or goal, even though there may be concerns which the counsellor is aware of that could be worked through. The autonomy and choice of the client to set the agenda and choose the issues to focus on or the goals they are working towards need to be honoured for the client not to be oppressed in the therapeutic process.

Reflection

Reflection as part of the internal emergent process in counselling may not be familiar to clients or may not be accessible for clients to utilize. The idea that the emergent process is an emotional process and works at emotional and relational depth, and is not a cognitive, intellectual or academic process, may be new to clients. It may be their first experience of engaging in an emotional and reflective process in counselling and if they find it difficult, they may reject or leave the counselling itself or request for a more directive or solution-oriented process.

Internal and external change

Internal changes are the shifts happening in the client's internal world, such as changes to their feelings, thoughts, understanding of their lived experiences, identity or the development of greater meaning-making in themselves. External changes are the shifts happening in the client's external 'out there' world, in their relationships, circumstances and experiences.

How does the client know that change has occurred? What is seen as change? Will a client have changed but not see it or not view it as change? Does the change feel small, therefore it doesn't look big or significant enough for them to see it as a big change? Are they dismissing changes that have happened internally or externally? What does a client see as a change that counts? Acknowledging that both internal and external change are important to identify, we can use reviews regularly to reflect on and support the client to identify and explore what they have noticed about themselves and what has changed for them since they started counselling.

Marginalized and minoritized clients

Marginalized and minoritized clients need particular focus on their external environment. Being located at the non-dominant oppressed end of the power relational dynamic has a particular impact on the client's sense of self and well-being as it leads to feelings of alienation.

How we work in exploring this experience of alienation with the client is to identify and understand:

- what is happening in the client's external world and relationships
- what is impacting on their internal world and mental health (is there an external cause to their distress?)
- the reality of making internal or external change
- what external changes can be made, only if they are within the client's control, ability, capacity and responsibility
- what internal changes can be made, only if they are within the client's control, ability, capacity and responsibility
- the client's external reality and its contributions to their internal world
- the internal and external causes of distress
- the client's current coping mechanisms (internally and externally)
- the client's experience of racial trauma and racial stress and explore how this may manifest for them
- holding the client's experience of alienation as their truth.

Endings

Endings, if viewed through an anti-oppressive lens, can be recognized and identified as the potential utilization of power (of the dominant counsellor) oppressing the non-dominant client. If there is a cultural distance between the counsellor and client, or the dominant counsellor, non-dominant client dynamic, the ending can be experienced by the client as the counsellor rejecting, abandoning and dismissing them. Who does the ending is utilizing their power, which is then interpreted, felt and experienced by the other based on their relational experiences 'out there' with dominant identities.

If the counsellor terminates counselling early (i.e. a premature ending), this may reinforce the client's feelings of not being good enough, failing the counselling itself, blaming themselves for it not working or not being understood by the counsellor, blaming themselves for the rejection or being dismissed based on their identity or an identity characteristic such as ethnicity or racialized identity. It is experienced as a repetition of how they are treated by professionals and services in this country, being minoritized, being dismissed or feeling unimportant and uncared for.

If the counsellor is introducing the ending, why end now? Has the goal been achieved? Do they feel they have reached their limit? Has a change occurred? Or instead, is it about ending due to feelings of helplessness or inadequacy from the counsellor, which are creating a power relational dynamic in which they are feeling powerless? Does the counsellor feel oppressed, shut down, marginalized, minimized or dismissed, and so needs to end the sessions?

Or perhaps the counsellor is doing the opposite and extending the contract, because they hold a power over the client, and can exploit the client for more hours and money? Is the counsellor 'hanging on' to clients because the client hasn't changed according to the counsellor's own agenda or expectations? What are these based on? The counsellor's own frame of reference, identity, worldview lens or culture? Is this also a power move over the client? Because the counsellor can, do they hold on to the client?

The experience of how the ending process is managed by the counsellor, whether that is a premature, sudden or expected ending, influences how the client will view the time spent together and the work done. Does the ending 'undo' the work of the counselling itself? Does the client feel betrayed, rejected or dismissed by the counsellor in the ending and so in return rejects or dismisses any work or progress achieved? Is this a way for the client to regain a level of power after being oppressed and marginalized by the oppressive counsellor?

The skill of working with endings in an anti-oppressive way is to acknowledge that the ending 'in here' may trigger feelings of and reactions to the client's experience of losses 'out there' or in their past experiences. Due to the external context for the client, does the client experience barriers, exclusions and rejections 'out there'? Where else have they felt excluded, dismissed or rejected? And how does the ending and loss of the therapeutic relationship and 'in here' mirror their experience? How will their experience and feelings of ending 'in here' help them to make meaning of their experiences and feelings of endings and losses 'out there'?

We need to acknowledge that the ending 'in here' may be the loss of a safe space for the client and when the client has experienced very few safe spaces 'out there', this loss is especially significant. This needs to be acknowledged and explored with the client, as the loss of a safe space and a safe person will have such an impact on them. It offers an opportunity for the client to explore their experience of a safe space and relationship, within the context and comparison of their 'out there' experiences and relationships.

Online counselling

There is a difference between face-to-face and online counselling in terms of establishing the therapeutic frame, boundaries, confidentiality and privacy. In face-to-face counselling, 100 per cent of the responsibility of establishing and maintaining the therapeutic frame, boundaries, privacy and confidentiality is held by the counsellor. In online counselling, we are handing the client their half of the responsibility for their privacy, boundaries, confidentiality and creation of the frame. What are the ethical issues for this? Can the client hold this responsibility? Are they aware and is it made explicit that they hold this responsibility or expectation? Where is this made clear in the contract?

Clients need to create their side of the therapeutic frame in their 'out there' space, which relocates the counselling from a separate space and entity when face to face and instead they must create the 'space' within their 'out there' space. The counselling moves from 'in here' to 'out there' and gets immersed or emerged into their 'out there' space, with the boundaries and frame possibly losing their clarity, firmness or robustness.

The challenge for collectivist-culture clients is to create a frame in their 'out there' space where they may already experience a lack of boundaries and privacy. When internally they may not have established boundaries in relationships, because of their collectivist sense of self as 'we', then establishing an external space 'out there' and creating a boundaried and private space for counselling becomes incredibly difficult. When it comes to contracting, how do we contract for online work? What do we need to consider when contracting with individualist and collectivist clients?

Reflective exercises

Thinking of your case study client, how does your client experience the process? What factors might you need to consider about the process when working with your client? What aspects of the process are more challenging for the client to use? What might you need to now include or add to the process in working with your client?

....

....

....

....

....

....

How has your client understood and approached the role of counselling? How has the client identified the goals and agenda for counselling? How might these reflect the client's identity?

....

....

....

....

....

....

How do you know that change has occurred for the client? How does the client know that change has occurred?

....

....

....

....

....

....

How might the client be experiencing alienation? What might you need to consider in how you work with the ending with your client?

....

....

....

....

....

....

What might you need to additionally consider if working online with your client? If they are a collectivist culture client, what else might you need to consider if working online?

....

....

....

....

....

....

Based on all your case study client reflections, how might you now work with the client? What would you do the same? What would you do differently? What would you need to add in or consider to be able to offer your client an anti-oppressive therapeutic process and relationship?

....

....

....

....

....

....

Part 3: Reflections

What are your thoughts, feelings and reflections on learning about the application of the Working within Diversity model in therapeutic practice?

....

....

....

....

....

....

In what ways does the application of the Working within Diversity model support or challenge how you currently approach your clinical practice?

....

....

....

....

....

....

What comes to mind when you think about what you need to change, do differently or think about differently in your therapeutic practice?

....

....

....

....

....

....

What might be some actions you can take moving forward, to be able to implement any aspect of the Working within Diversity model in your therapeutic practice?

....

....

....

....

....

....

PART 4

Working within Diversity in Reflective Practice

In Part 4, I will present the application of the Working within Diversity model to clinical/therapeutic supervision practice, including the consultation (supervision of supervision) practice, how to develop anti-oppressive, reflective supervision and supervisory relationships and how to develop an anti-oppressive approach to reflective self-care practice.

CHAPTER 17

Supervision

In this chapter, I will present the application of the Working within Diversity model to supervision by exploring and introducing you to a new anti-oppressive supervision model.

Please note that the model and approach includes its application to supervision of supervision (which is named here as 'consultation'), so that we can continue to offer an anti-oppressive lens to our reflective practice in all therapeutic, supervisory and consultation professional relationships and reflective processes that we engage in across all levels of our clinical practice. Therefore, everything that is set out in this chapter is equally applicable to supervision and supervision relationships (between counsellor/supervisee and supervisor) and consultation and consultation relationships (between supervisor and consultant). Where supervision or supervision relationship is referred to, this will also include its application to the consultation relationship, if it has not been explicitly stated. The supervision relationship triangles (Figure 23) illustrate the three-way nature of the supervision and consultation relationship dynamic.

It can be challenging to engage in supervision through an intersectional lens, whether you are the supervisee, supervisor or consultant (supervisor of supervisors). It requires openness, open dialogue, honesty, vulnerability and authenticity, as well as developing cultural attunement to your clients or supervisees, to be able to acknowledge your own power and privilege, as well as to identify your ability to oppress others. It may be more comfortable and therefore easier to identify your oppressed experiences and defend against, deny or avoid the privileged parts of your identity.

To be able to engage in and start to take up a position of openness, open dialogue, honesty, vulnerability and authenticity in supervision, there are some steps you can take as a supervisee, supervisor or consultant:

- Name your own intersectional identity.
- In supervision: name the client's intersectionality and how this helps both the supervisee and supervisor to understand the client's lived experience, social location and experience of privilege and oppression.
- In consultation: name the counsellor's intersectionality and how this helps both the supervisor and consultant to understand the counsellor's lived experience, social location and experience of privilege and oppression.

The Identity Wheel tool (Figures 3 and 4) and the Scales of Power in Identity Characteristics tool (Figures 12 and 13) can be used to identify the intersectional identities of the clients, counsellor and supervisor.

As a supervisor, these are ways you can approach the process:

- Support your supervisee's understanding of intersectionality and how power, privilege and oppression can be held and utilized within our identities and relationships, and in our therapeutic and supervision relationships.
- Help the supervisee to explore their own intersectional identity and understand their own power and privilege held in their identity.
- Identify how the two identities and intersectionalities of the counsellor and client stack up against each other in the therapeutic relationship and who holds power and how they may each repeat their use of power or experience of oppression in the therapeutic relationship. The Scales of Relational Power tool can be used to identify both the counsellor and client's privileged and oppressed identities (Figure 20).
- Explore how the client and supervisee's intersectional identity may impact on their therapeutic process and relationship, what barriers it may create and how to make it a safe space for the client.
- Explore which identity characteristic(s) is being brought into the therapeutic relationship first and what is being prioritized by the client in their identity.
- Explore how close or distant the two identities are with one another.
- Ask if there is an unconscious 'othering' or an over-identification happening between them? How similar or distant are their intersectionalities and experiences of privilege or oppression?
- Identify if any power-oppression dynamic is being repeated consciously/unconsciously in their relationship.

As the supervisee, the above points can also support you in your reflections and processing of your clinical practice and each client session, as well as supporting you in your preparation for effective supervision.

As the consultant, the same above points for supervision apply to the consultant process, but instead of exploring the client and supervisee's intersectional identities and focusing on the therapeutic relationship, we are exploring the supervisee and supervisor's intersectional identities and focusing on the supervision relationship. The two supervision and consultation three-way triangular relationships are depicted in Figure 23.

In the 'in here' supervision space and relationship, oppression can be experienced through the lack of creating safe spaces, so it's important to recognize, understand and know how to create a safe space for both you and your supervisee. This is influenced by your intersectional identities and if either or both of you experience spaces as unsafe 'out there', and whether this is being repeated and applied in the supervision relationship. This can initially be done by having a contract in place, so the supervisee knows the frame and boundaries of the work you'll be doing together, but also through dialogue by asking what would support your supervisee to feel safe in the 'in here' supervision space.

By identifying the intersectional identities of supervisor, supervisee and clients, you can acknowledge each person's power, privilege and experiences of oppression and how the power dynamics and relationships experienced 'out there', for supervisee and supervisor, may get re-created in supervision relationships. This may show up as the supervisee's identity and experiences being oppressed through marginalization and minimization by the supervisor (which would re-create the power-oppression dynamic) or parts of the supervisor's identity and relational dynamic being split off, missed, denied or ignored.

We also need to recognize how the supervisor and supervisee relate to the space. Do they end the space or relationship to shut down or avoid any process or exploration of power and oppression? Is there avoidance to challenge, bring something challenging or name something challenging and so collude to move away from it? What is being missed or not spoken about because it conflicts with privileged and oppressed parts of the supervisor's identity or with the supervisor and supervisee's parts of identity? What space is given to supervisees to think about issues or make decisions or does the supervisor's power lead to dictating a decision or outcome to the supervisee? So, it's important that you're able to acknowledge the impact of your intersectional identity on your supervisory relationships and work towards creating a supervision relationship in which the power is both acknowledged and flattened, and that you identify where the power may be re-enacted and re-experienced 'in here'.

Supervision needs to meet the needs of supervisees at their current level of experience and those needs must be matched and met by the right supervisor. An experienced supervisor doesn't automatically mean that they are the best supervisor for the supervisee. Paramount to the relationship is the inclusion and promoting of equality between supervisor and supervisee, where equality is about both people being seen, being transparent, engaging in the process and relationship and thriving in the supervision work. It is not about the supervisee being oppressed, marginalized and minoritized by an oppressive, dominant supervisor who uses their power as the expert or in an authority position and pushes a supervisee into an oppressive survival position in the process and the relationship.

Below are some examples of what would constitute oppressive supervision practice, where supervisors abuse their power and privilege against and over the supervisee:

- Telling supervisees what to do.
- Not allowing supervisees to bring all of themselves into the supervision space.
- Telling supervisees to work with a client they don't feel competent to work with.
- Not acknowledging that the supervisee has outgrown the supervisor.
- Not allowing supervisees to grow.
- Preventing supervisees from finding a new supervisor.
- Pushing supervisees into positions of powerlessness, oppression or dependency on the supervisor (i.e. needs supervisor to write a report to pass the course/accreditation).
- Not being able to work with the difference if there is a poor match between supervisor and supervisee's modality or mixed-modality supervision group.
- Forcing their modality onto the supervisee and supervision process.
- Expecting the supervisee to take their advice and apply it in their counselling relationships.

Instead, we can challenge ourselves as supervisors to offer an anti-oppressive approach to supervision by taking up the position of mentor, cheerleader and supporter for our supervisees. They can, will and need to outgrow us. We need to support our supervisees' growth and transformation in their professional and clinical development, work holistically to address and identify their potential, be a reflective resource, explore clinical issues and offer both high challenge and high support in the process and relationally.

Looking through an anti-oppressive lens, we need to understand the concepts of – and how to work therapeutically with – identity, lived experiences, diversity, power and privilege dynamics within systems of oppression, two intersectional identities present in therapeutic relationships. We need to create safe supervisory spaces and relationships, take on the responsibility to use and educate ourselves on anti-oppressive language, support supervisees' understanding of language (otherwise it's oppressive if the supervisor has the language but the supervisee doesn't have it) and model and explore an anti-oppressive supervisory relationship and therapeutic relationships.

Figure 23: The supervision relationship triangles

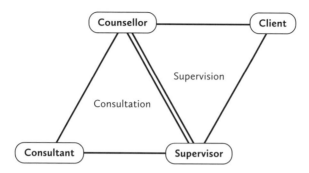

An anti-oppressive supervision model would include how intersectionality and intersectional identities can be identified and understood, how power can be flattened in the supervision and therapeutic relationships, how systemic oppression is identified and understood as being played out relationally for each person, and how we can use a systemic, cultural, social, political and historical lens to look at the overall supervisory and therapeutic processes taking place.

The 'Nine-Eyed' Anti-Oppressive Supervision Model, presented below (Figure 24) adapts the 'seven-eyed' model of supervision by Hawkins and Shohet (2000) for the three-way triangular supervisory relationships of supervisor-supervisee-client and consultant-supervisor-supervisee (Figure 23) and looks at these relationships through an anti-oppressive lens. This model includes what the supervisor must consider not only in offering supervision to their supervisee but also in their own supervision of supervision (i.e. the supervisor's consultation), which is often overlooked in considering the wider clinical supervision process.

> **Eye 1:** Client's intersectional identity and lived experience – the client's life and experiences, including exploration of their intersectional identity and how they are oppressed; where they hold power and privilege; and what intersectional identity differences and similarities there are between client and counsellor.

> **Eye 2:** Counsellor's therapeutic interventions – interventions, techniques and strategies used by the counsellor in the counselling session with the client, including understanding how the counsellor's identity influences their interventions; what assumptions are being made; how different or outside the client's world or frame of reference they feel and so how might they be responding to the client from their own frame of reference, philosophy and culture.

Figure 24: Anti-Oppressive Nine-Eyed Supervision Model

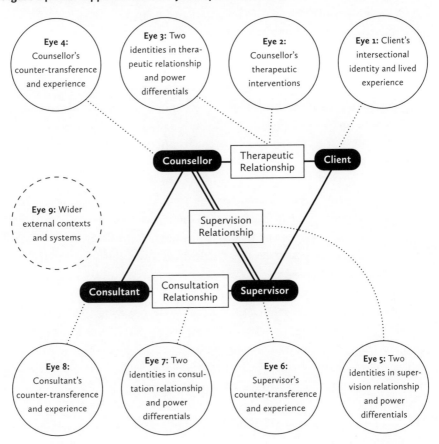

Eye 3: Two identities in therapeutic relationship – exploring the therapeutic relationship, including how their intersectional identities relate to one another; awareness of power differentials; how they 'other' each other; how their power and privilege are used and how they oppress, minimize or marginalize one another; if they are a culturally close or culturally distant counsellor-client match; what potential there is for collusion or over-identification if culturally close and/or avoidance or denial if culturally distant.

Eye 4: Counsellor's counter-transference and experience – the counsellor's counter-transference, including understanding when, how and why they want to oppress or feel oppressed by the client; where counter-transference feelings, experiences or the client's narrative are split off and marginalized; where power is being used; and how the transference is being played out to repeat an oppressed and unequal relationship.

Eye 5: Two identities in supervision relationship – exploring the supervision relationship, as the therapeutic relationship, including how their intersectional identities relate to one another; awareness of power differentials; how they 'other' each other; how their power and privilege are used; how they oppress, minimize or marginalize one another and how this may be a parallel process of the therapeutic relationship; if they are a culturally close or culturally distant supervisor-supervisee match and what potential there is for collusion or over-identification if culturally close, and/or avoidance or denial if culturally distant; and how they might collude with systems of oppression for them both to marginalize, minoritize or oppress the client.

Eye 6: Supervisor's counter-transference and experience – the supervisor's counter-transference, including understanding when, how and why they want to oppress or feel oppressed by supervisee or client; where counter-transference feelings and experiences or the client's narrative are split off and marginalized; where power is being used and how the transference is being played out to repeat an oppressed and unequal relationship with the supervisee; understanding how the supervisor's identity influences their interventions; what assumptions are being made; how different or outside the supervisee and client's world or frame of reference they feel and so how they might be responding to the supervisee and client from their own frame of reference, philosophy and culture; and if there is a parallel process of the counsellor's counter-transference.

Eye 7: Two identities in consultation relationship – exploring the consultation relationship (supervision of supervision), between the supervisor and their supervisor (consultant), as the therapeutic and supervision relationships, including how their intersectional identities relate to one another; awareness of power differentials; how they 'other' each other; how their power and privilege are used and how they oppress, minimize or marginalize one another and how this may be a parallel process of the therapeutic and/or supervision relationship; if they are a culturally close or culturally distant consultant-supervisor match and what potential there is for collusion or over-identification if culturally close, and/or avoidance or denial if culturally distant; and how they might collude with systems of oppression for them both to marginalize, minoritize or oppress the counsellor and/or clients.

Eye 8: Consultant's counter-transference and experience – the consultant's counter-transference, including understanding when, how and why they want to oppress or feel oppressed by the supervisor or counsellor; where counter-transference feelings and experiences or the supervisor or counsellor's narrative are split off and marginalized; where power is being used and how the transference is being played out to repeat an oppressed and unequal relationship with the supervisor; how the consultant's identity influences their interventions; what assumptions are being made; how different or outside the supervisor and counsellor's world or frame of reference they feel and so how they might be responding to the supervisor and counsellor from their own frame of reference, philosophy and culture, and if there is a parallel process of the supervisor's counter-transference.

Eye 9: Wider external contexts – the wider external context and system, including the cultural, social-political and systemic contexts of our experiences and how they influence and shape our lived experiences and sense of self/identity, recognizing the systemic oppression and inequalities which exist 'out there' and form the context and framework for all our work and relationships.

This anti-oppressive model adds the external, social, cultural, political, historical and structural contexts back into the counselling, supervision and consultation settings and content, by identifying and working with intersectional identities and their impact on therapeutic, supervisory and consultation relationships, and understanding the lived experiences through and within these contexts.

Naming and identifying our intersectional identity in the supervision and consultation relationships (as consultant, supervisor, supervisee and client's identities) helps us to identify the differences among us and how we each experience the world through and because of our social position and the power and oppression we experience.

Adding in and working with identity and intersectionality within the supervision context allows the lived experiences and social positions of clients, supervisees, supervisors and consultants to be contextualized and helps us understand how power and oppression may be played out and re-enacted within therapeutic, supervisory and consultation relationships and in parallel to one another. There is an obvious role power and privilege held by consultants, supervisors and counsellors, positioning them as 'experts' with credibility and so holding influence (in therapeutic/supervision relationships) over supervisees and clients.

Paying attention to the power and oppression inequality in consultation, supervision and therapeutic relationships enables us to identify where power and oppression exist and how they get enacted, so that we can address their enactment and work out how to rebalance and flatten the power between everyone. Consciously or unconsciously supervisors, supervisees and clients can face oppression in their relationships, as consultants, supervisors and counsellors in their 'helper' role can use their power and privilege to oppress, marginalize, deny and devalue the experiences, feelings, thoughts and content of what the supervisor/supervisee/ client brings to the session. They can dominate or over-power with their own opinion, which could be perceived as colonizing the narrative (taking ownership of it). In return, supervisors, supervisees and clients can collude with their marginalization by feeling unable to challenge, to voice their opinions or disagree, as they are in the less powerful position of 'helpee' and are vulnerable because they need help from the consultant/supervisor/counsellor.

Both power and oppression can be present at the same time. While power and privilege can mean power over the other, there are also experiences of oppression in the same relationships, such as where you both experience similar oppressions (where your oppressions meet) or where you experience your own but different oppressions (where your oppressions don't meet) or where you might miss each other's oppressions as they are blind spots or unconscious to you and your own experiences of oppression (what oppressions may get missed).

We need to recognize that the supervisor, supervisee and client are responsible, capable, have agency and autonomy and are also in need of help and support. We need to be aware of how our power can be present, how we use our role power, what language we use, how we may relate to the supervisor/supervisee and how we work with and treat their narrative, material and lived experiences, while keeping in mind how the supervisor/supervisee may relate back and position themselves and enact the position of oppressed towards us as the consultant/supervisor. To pay attention and work with oppressions in consultant and supervision relationships is to ask yourself, where do we meet, where don't we meet and where do we miss each other?

Reflective exercises

What are your thoughts, feelings and reflections on learning about the application of the Working within Diversity model to supervision or consultant (either as a supervisee, supervisor or consultant)?

....

....

....

....

....

....

In what ways does the application of the Working within Diversity model support or challenge how you currently approach your supervision practice (either as a supervisee, supervisor or consultant)?

....

....

....

....

....

....

What comes to mind when you think about what you need to change, do differently or think about differently in your supervision practice (either as a supervisee, supervisor or consultant)?

....

....

....

....

....

....

What might be some actions you can take moving forward, to be able to implement any aspect of the Working within Diversity model in your supervision practice (either as a supervisee, supervisor or consultant)?

....

....

....

....

....

....

CHAPTER 18

Self-Care

In this chapter, we will explore and reflect on self-care as a practice and the needs this meets, alongside a new anti-oppressive approach to self-care. I will invite you to reflect on your current self-care practice and there will be an opportunity to create an anti-oppressive self-care plan for yourself moving forward.

Let us start with reflecting on how you currently think about and practice self-care.

Reflective exercises

What are your initial or immediate thoughts when you think of the phrase 'self-care'? What are some of your beliefs about self-care?

....

....

....

....

....

....

....

....

What do you do for your self-care? Is self-care part of your daily or weekly routine? Do you have a self-care plan or not?

....

....

....

....

....

....

If you practise self-care, what needs are being met? What needs are being missed and not met?

....

....

....

....

....

....

The phrase 'self-care' can conjure up all sorts of images and quite often is stereotyped and depicted as the practice of self-care as a bubble bath or reading a book curled up on the sofa with a hot mug of tea. Now while these are absolutely a form of self-care practice for some, it's important that we really understand what self-care is, what needs it is meeting and whether our self-care practice is working for us.

Self-care is the practice of meeting needs through self-directed actions, behaviours and thoughts. We can often focus on the practice of self-care without really understanding or easily identifying the needs which are being met through the practice. If you were to search for self-care plans on the internet, you would be shown many which identify seven types of needs we have, with many examples of how to meet them. The seven needs are: emotional, spiritual, mental, psychological, personal, physical and professional needs.

What are your initial thoughts about these seven needs? Were you aware of all seven needs? Do any surprise you as needs? Are some of them needs you haven't considered before?

....

....

....

....

....

....

How does your current self-care meet these seven needs? How intentional are you in meeting these seven needs? Are some needs met more often or easily than others? Are some needs neglected or ignored?

....

....

....

....

....

....

The Art of Flowfilment

In understanding what self-care is and the needs they meet, in early 2020 I presented my Ted Talk on 'The Art of Flowfilment' (Khan, 2020). I repositioned self-care as the 'flowfilment' (flow and fulfilment) of energy in and out of us. In understanding that self-care is the practice of receiving good and healthy energy flowing into us and being fulfilled, replenished and nurtured by that energy, while implementing boundaries against energy that is unhealthy for us, we can begin to say that we are cultivating the 'art of flowfilment' in our self-care.

When self-care becomes a focus on the flow and fulfilment (flowfilment) of energy, then we can ask ourselves what we are doing to fill ourselves up with good energy. Are we feeling fulfilled, replenished and nurtured through this? Are we experiencing 'flowfilment'? Are our needs being met through these self-care practices? Is self-care working for us?

Reflective exercises

How does the concept of 'flowfilment' complement or conflict with your self-care practice? Do you feel that your self-care is making you feel fulfilled and replenished?

....

....

....

....

....

....

If your self-care is reflective of flowfilment, which of your needs are being met? Are some of your needs being met more easily than others?

....

....

....

....

....

....

An anti-oppressive approach to self-care

Being a reflective anti-oppressive practitioner, by applying the Working within Diversity model and approach and engaging in an anti-oppressive practice with your clients and supervisees, requires you to be open, vulnerable, authentic and honest with yourself. To engage with this book's content and its reflective exercises and to grow as a practitioner, I invite you to offer yourself self-care in a way that supports your personal and professional growth, recognizes and honours all parts of you and meets all your needs. These are the parts of you that you lead with, that hold power, and that experience oppression and how you are treated as a majority or minoritized and marginalized person. It is also the parts that you oppress, push away, deny and ignore; the parts that you recognize as your strengths and show the world; the parts you label as weak or vulnerable, the 'not so good' or 'bad' parts of you, and the parts you push away, keep hidden and don't care for.

If you've engaged in the reflective exercises, you may have come across some of these deeper, hidden, denied or unknown parts of you, perhaps parts that you were not so happy to recognize and identify. Self-care is not about making it all better but about honouring our whole self, intersectional identity and lived experiences with self-compassion. It is recognizing and sitting with our fullness; looking after all those parts; identifying what each part needs from us.

We recognize that our lived experiences and how we are related to and treated is due to our intersectional identity, so we each experience the world in a unique way. We are left feeling a particular way about our self, identity, relationships and sense of place in the world. Therefore, what we need to do for our self-care is not only to take care of our needs and each part of ourselves internally, with self-compassion, self-esteem, self-value and self-respect, but also to recognize that self-care is what we need to do externally in the world, in relationships and in spaces we engage in. Anti-oppressive self-care therefore includes the addition of an eighth need – our social and relational needs – alongside our other seven needs (emotional, spiritual, mental, psychological, personal, physical and professional needs).

The self-care we practise needs to be for all parts of our identity, self and lived experiences, for both our oppressor/privileged parts and oppressed/minoritized parts.

The self-care practised for our privileged identities is equally important and needed, as engaging in anti-oppressive practice and reflecting on our power, privilege and opportunities to (consciously or unconsciously) oppress others requires a level of self-compassion to be able to sit with ourselves authentically, vulnerably and honestly.

Self-care for our minoritized identities looks, feels and lands differently. For those who are visibly or dominantly at the minoritized and oppressed end of the spectrum, to offer ourselves self-care when we are being located, treated and related to as a 'minority', as less than, becomes an act of social justice, an act of equality, an act of value and self-worth against the dominant high social status identity groups that locate and relate to us as low social status. Taking care of ourselves is everything when we are being seen, treated and told that we are not worthy of it. For anyone who is minoritized, self-care challenges the 'norm', asking us not to collude in the undervaluing, marginalizing, oppressing and dismissing of ourselves, of our needs, of our own worth, value and equality. Self-care sends the very important message that we are valuable, and worthy of being taken care of.

The boundaries we put in place in our relationships and in spaces we engage in are vital to our survival of the trauma of being subjected to oppression, power, privilege, bias and prejudice, and the myriad of ways we can be minoritized and marginalized.

The self-care we practise can also be challenging because it is a relationship dynamic of our self, caring for and meeting the needs of our self. The basis of self-care is that it is a relationship with our individual internal and external self, which reflects an individualist 'I' culture sense of self and identity. To practise self-care prioritizes a self that is an 'I', with clear boundaries between self and others, and we are able to identify our self as an individual and our individual needs. On the other hand, a collectivist 'we' sense of self holds a group or family identity and so makes it more challenging to identify what a person's individual needs are and how to meet them, as self-care asks the person to move from a 'we' self and identity to an individualist 'I' self and identity. This shift in identity and focus on the individual self challenges not only the relationship you may have with yourself and your collective 'we' group, but also how to meet and prioritize your individual needs.

These are the essential elements of anti-oppressive self-care:

- Identifying your beliefs about self-care and their influence on your practice of self-care.
- Identifying how your beliefs about self-care reflect your intersectional identity, sense of self and values about yourself.
- Understanding that you are building an anti-oppressive relationship with all parts of yourself.
- Recognizing that it is about the quality and equality of relationship you have with yourself and taking care of and meeting the needs of all parts of you – every aspect of your lived experiences and intersectional identity.
- Identifying how you hold and utilize internalized oppression towards yourself by oppressing, denying, ignoring, dismissing, minimizing and marginalizing any part of you or any need you have.
- Identifying how you oppress yourself through marginalizing, minimizing, dismissing and devaluing your own self or sense of self and identity.
- Identifying the struggles and challenges of practising self-care because of internalized beliefs or a sense of self, which places yourself secondary or last to other people and their needs. This is especially true and challenging for

collectivist 'we' culture people, whose sense of self as a 'we' can challenge and conflict with a practice of self-care that prioritizes the self as an 'I'.

- Recognizing if your sense of self is placed within an individualist 'I' sense of self or a collectivist 'we' sense of self, and which one then influences how much you can prioritize and practise self-care.
- Respecting all eight needs and implementing an intentional anti-oppressive self-care plan to practise self-care, which will fully meet all your eight needs.

Reflective exercises

If you practise self-care, do you feel that it is an anti-oppressive approach, which takes care of all of you, or do you now recognize that it is an oppressive approach, which only takes care of parts of you and denies or ignores other parts of you or needs you have?

....

....

....

....

....

....

If you don't have an intentional self-care plan, why is that? What is stopping you – an external power or an internalized oppression? What are your initial thoughts and responses in picturing a self-care plan or practising self-care? Are those thoughts and responses self-compassionate or are they oppressive?

....

....

....

....

....

....

Does your self-care practice reflect your identity or an identity characteristic – either through a dominant/privileged or minoritized identity? Does your self-care practice reflect your cultural sense of self as an individualist 'I' or collectivist 'we'? How does that create challenges or difficulties in practising self-care? How does it create ease in practising self-care?

....

....

....

....

....

....

Based on what self-care you may be currently practising, does your self-care feel fulfilling? Does your self-care meet your needs? If yes, why and how does it meet your needs? If no, why doesn't it meet your needs? What is missing or what is it that you are not doing enough of or too much of?

....

....

....

....

....

....

Safe spaces and groups for self-care

Self-care is often mistaken as an individual exercise, to be done alone or in isolation. Many of our needs are met socially, in community, in relationship and through connection with others. We need social and relational self-care practices to meet our social-relational need, but through social activities we can meet many of our other needs too. These sit in a complementary way alongside our internal and individual self-care activities.

Reflective exercises

What safe social spaces or groups do you have access to, to support your self-care? To support your professional development? To support your growth as an anti-oppressive practitioner?

....

....

....

....

....

....

What safe relationships and groups do you have access to? Do you feel connected to others? Do you feel you have a support team or network around you that you can go to? If you do, what has made it a safe space and relational group for you? If you don't, what would a safe group look like for you? What would you like from that group?

....

....

....

....

....

....

Who do you need to connect to? Do you feel that you need to build up your social and relational spaces and groups? Do you need to build a team around you? Do you need more allies in your team? Do you need to access more culturally close groups and spaces? Do you need more safe spaces and groups? What groups might you need to source or create? What do you need to do to find more safe spaces and groups?

....

....

....
....
....
....

Microaffirmations

In direct contrast and challenge to the microaggressions you may face daily, microaffirmations, as a form of daily self-care, affirm, validate and honour your own identity and lived experiences from a position of openness and transparency. They are daily, consistent and regular affirmations of yourself, your identity and your truth.

Reflective exercises

What are the ways in which you currently receive and accept microaffirmations (affirmations of your identity and lived experiences) every day?

....
....
....
....
....
....

What can you do to affirm your emotions, feelings and emotional reactions in their fullest expression, without minimizing, dismissing or ignoring how you feel?

....
....

....

....

....

....

What can you do to affirm, acknowledge and honour your daily experiences? How can you capture, contain and hold your experiences without downplaying or making them 'smaller' and oppressing yourself? How do you honour your life in its fullest experience?

....

....

....

....

....

....

Anti-oppressive self-care plan

In thinking about your self-care and what you might need to implement moving forward, it can be useful to create a self-care plan to identify what you need, what you need to do differently and what you need to add to your current self-care to feel replenished and nurtured in every aspect of yourself.

Activity: Answering the reflective questions below and filling in the Self-Care Wheel (Figure 26) can help to identify what types of self-care you are already engaging in, where needs might not be getting met and where there are gaps in your self-care. A template of the Anti-Oppressive Self-Care Wheel tool is also included in the online Appendix. Some examples have been provided in Figure 25; however, it is essential to recognize that self-care is about you meeting your specific and individual needs, which may not look the same as anyone else's and what they might need. This is an opportunity to recognize what your needs are and what you can do to support yourself in meeting your needs.

From the Anti-Oppressive Self-Care Wheels (Figures 25 and 26) you will notice that there are eight different categories of self-care needs that we each need to identify and meet through our self-care practice. In the anti-oppressive approach, I have added social and relational needs as additional aspects of our self-care, especially for us to be able to consider which social and relational spaces, people and groups are safe or unsafe for us and what types of safe spaces we need to nurture for ourselves. This is particularly important as you move forward in developing and engaging in anti-oppressive practice and becoming an anti-oppressive practitioner.

Reflective exercises

What do you picture as good, healthy or fulfilling self-care for you? What needs do you need to get met, which may not be currently met?

....

....

....

....

....

....

Moving forward as an anti-oppressive practitioner, what are your needs? To be able to do this work? To be able to grow, develop and feel supported in your work?

....

....

....

....

....

....

How will you meet these needs? What do you need to do for yourself?

....

....

....

....

....

....

What do you need to do differently in your self-care practice? What do you need more time and space for?

....

....

....

....

....

....

What do you need to add to your self-care practice? What do you need to make time and space for? What is currently missing in your self-care?

....

....

....

....

....

....

Figure 25: Anti-Oppressive Self-Care Wheel with examples

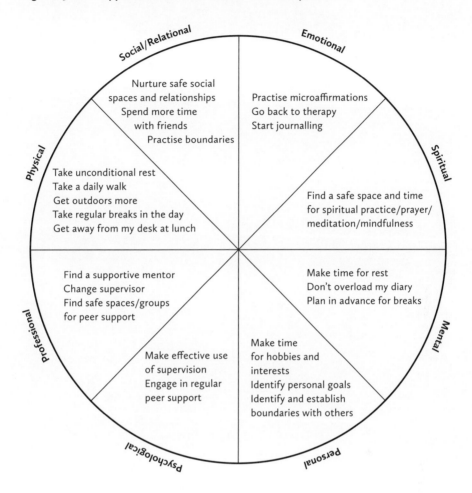

Figure 26: Anti-Oppressive Self-Care Wheel (template)

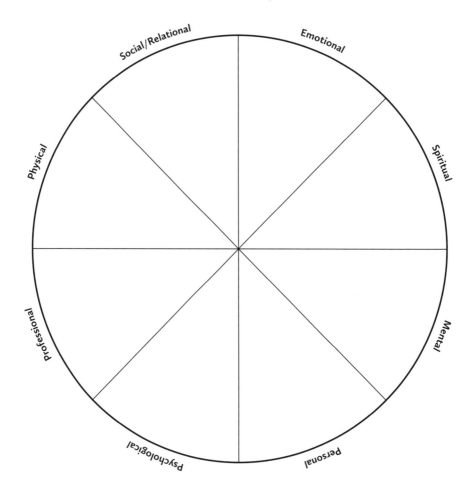

Final reflections

Looking back at where you started, re-read your answers to the reflective questions at the start of Part 1.

What are your immediate thoughts, reflections and feelings about what you wrote then?

....

....

....

....

....

....

....

What has changed, shifted or developed since then? What does anti-oppressive practice mean to you now? What do you think it looks like in practice now?

....

....

....

....

....

....

....

What changes have occurred within you since you started to read through this workbook? What have you noticed?

....

....

....

....

....

....

....

What has come to your attention? What are you now paying attention to? What needs paying attention to? What will you implement, change or add to your clinical practice and professional work, because of the Working within Diversity model and its anti-oppressive approach?

....

....

....

....

....

....

CHAPTER 19

Moving Forward in Anti-Oppressive Practice

For practitioners

Now that you have read and worked through this reflective guide on anti-oppressive practice, my intentions and hope for you, as a practitioner, are that you have been able to gain some new learning, reflections and perspectives from this process. I invite you to apply these to your practice, to your supervision and self-care, and to your continued development and reflection as an anti-oppressive practitioner. I invite you to identify your learning from this reflective guide, to recognize, name and pinpoint where and how you can change and adapt your work to readdress inequalities, offer equality and apply the Working within Diversity model and its principles into your work and reflective practice moving forward. Lastly, I would like to encourage you to make a commitment to Working within Diversity, its five components and seven principles and its anti-oppressive approach. I urge you to commit to the learning, growth, reading, reflection, internal work and development that come with embodying anti-oppressive practice in your work, and in best ethical, socially just therapeutic and clinical practice. Below, I have reiterated the commitments listed in Chapter 2, under 'Principle 2: Systemic, structural and social inequalities and oppressions'. Can you make the commitment to them?

- Recognizing and acknowledging the impact of systemic, structural and social inequalities.
- Recognizing and acknowledging identity and intersectional identities and their impact on people's lived experiences.
- Recognizing and acknowledging the impact of systems of oppressions and the use of power, privilege and oppression in relational dynamics, which also continue to uphold the supremacy of dominant identity groups and societies.

- Being proactively involved in anti-oppressive practice, in its development, in our ongoing learning and in its application to our work and profession.
- Not proactively engaging in oppressive practices, leaving us in the position of passivity, indifference, unawareness or inaction, which reflects a dominant, oppressive attitude and continues to uphold and indicate our support of current systemic inequalities and power-oppressive relational dynamics without challenging them.

For therapy/counselling/therapeutic practice training institutions, courses and tutors

Now that you have read and worked through this reflective guide on anti-oppressive practice, my intentions and hope for you, as a tutor or part of a training institution, are that you have been able to gain some new learning, reflections or perspectives from this process. I invite you to recognize and identify where that learning or growth can be added to, adapted and used in the delivery of training courses and the content of those courses.

To all training institutions and tutors, I invite you to add and embed anti-oppressive practice and the Working within Diversity model and its principles into your curriculums, courses and teaching approaches, as a training standard, to teach ethical and socially just anti-oppressive practice. I encourage the learning, development and support of tutors and course leads to engage in the reflective learning and content throughout this book, alongside my workshops and training courses on Working within Diversity and anti-oppressive practice. I welcome the use of this reflective guide, the Working within Diversity model and its anti-oppressive approach as a curriculum and training resource for institutions, courses, tutors and their students. I also welcome the invitation from institutions and tutors to deliver my Working within Diversity model and anti-oppressive approach to practice, to students and for 'train the trainer/tutor' programmes across all levels of the profession.

For the profession

My intentions and hope for the profession are that with this reflective guide, and its brand-new Working within Diversity model and approach to anti-oppressive practice, there is new understanding of the therapeutic work delivered to clients and supervisees, including the external contexts within which that practice is delivered. I invite the profession to recognize the importance of integrating Working within

Diversity and anti-oppressive practice into the core of our work, as a professional training and ethical standard within our frameworks, good practice guidelines, qualifications and practice at all levels. I invite the profession to move to understanding, embodying and championing socially just, anti-oppressive practice and for this to be at the heart of delivering ethical therapeutic practice to clients and supervisees. This needs to be a thread running through all aspects and levels of the profession – clinical practice, supervision, training and continuous development. I welcome new and continued conversations and discussions alongside genuine action that demonstrate the much-needed structural and systemic changes required in our profession. This includes changes to our professional standards, training pathways, courses and therapeutic practices in order to offer Working within Diversity and anti-oppressive practice, which honours and relates to all within and engaging with the profession ethically and equally.

Reflective exercise

Note down any thoughts, hopes, actions and intentions you have for moving forward to Working within Diversity and offering anti-oppressive practice in any of your roles:

Further Reading

Below is a selection of suggested further reading on the topics covered in this book.

Ababio, B. & Littlewood, R. (eds) (2019) *Intercultural Therapy*. Abingdon: Routledge.

Agarwal, P. (2020) *Sway: Unravelling Unconscious Bias*. London: Bloomsbury.

Bhopal, K. (2018) *White Privilege: The Myth of a Post-Racial Society*. Bristol: Policy Press.

Collins, P. H. & Bilge, S. (2016) *Intersectionality*. Cambridge: Polity Press.

Daniels, S. (2022) *The Anti-Racist Organization*. Chichester: John Wiley & Sons.

Dottolo, A.L. & Kaschak, E. (eds) (2016) *Whiteness and White Privilege in Psychotherapy*. Abingdon: Routledge.

Eberhardt, J.L. (2019) *Biased*. London: Penguin.

Ellis, E. (2021) *The Race Conversation*. London: Confer Books.

Fakhry Davids, M. (2011) *Internal Racism*. Basingstoke: Palgrave Macmillan.

Hook, J.N., Davis, D., Owen, J. & DeBlaere, C. (2017) *Cultural Humility*. Washington: American Psychological Association.

Kendi, I.X. (2019) *How to be an Antiracist*. London: Bodley Head.

McKenzie-Mavinga, I. (2009) *Black Issues in the Therapeutic Process*. Basingstoke: Palgrave Macmillan.

McKenzie-Mavinga, I. (2016) *The Challenge of Racism in Therapeutic Practice*. London: Palgrave.

Menakem, R. (2021) *My Grandmother's Hands*. London: Penguin.

Romera, M. (2018) *Introducing Intersectionality*. Cambridge: Polity Press.

Saad, L.F. (2020) *Me and White Supremacy*. London: Quercus.

Tuckwell, G. (2002) *Racial Identity, White Counsellors and Therapists*. Buckingham: Open University Press.

Turner, D. (2021) *Intersections of Privilege and Otherness in Counselling and Psychotherapy*. Abingdon: Routledge.

References

Cameron, R. (2020) *Working with Difference and Diversity in Counselling and Psychotherapy*. London: Sage Publications.

Chinook Fund (2015) *General Terms and Forms of Oppression*. https://chinookfund.org/wp-content/uploads/2015/10/Supplemental-Information-for-Funding-Guidelines.pdf.

Crenshaw, K. (1989) *What Is Intersectionality?* https://youtu.be/ViDtnfQ9FHc (uploaded 22 June 2018).

D'Ardenne, P. & Mahtani, A. (1989) *Transcultural Counselling in Action*. London: Sage Publications.

Eddo-Lodge, R. (2017) *Why I'm No Longer Talking to White People About Race*. London: Bloomsbury Publishing.

Eleftheriadou, Z. (1994) *Transcultural Counselling*. London: Central Book Publishing.

Gilbert, P. & Procter, S. (2006) Compassionate mind training for people with high shame and self-criticism. *Clinical Psychology and Psychotherapy*, 13, 353–379.

Hawkins, P. & Shohet, R. (2000) *Supervision in the Helping Professions (second edition)*. Buckingham: Open University Press.

Hofstede, G., Hofstede G.J. & Monkov, M. (2010) *Cultures and Organizations: Software of the Mind*. New York, NY: McGraw-Hill.

Johnstone, L. & Boyle, M. with Cromby, J., Dillon, J. *et al.* (2018) *The Power Threat Meaning Framework: Overview*. Leicester: British Psychological Society.

Karpman, S. (1968) Fairy tales and script drama analysis. *Transactional Analysis Bulletin*, 7(26), 39–43.

Khan, M. (2020) *Grow to Glow: The Art of Flowfilment*. TEDx Talk. www.ted.com/talks/myira_khan_grow_to_glow_the_art_of_flowfilment.

Lago, C. (1996) *Race, Culture and Counselling*. Maidenhead: Open University Press.

McIntosh, P. (1989) White privilege: Unpacking the invisible knapsack. *Peace and Freedom Magazine* (July/August 10/12).

Proctor, G. (2017) *The Dynamics of Power (second edition)*. Monmouth: PCCS Books.

Thomas, A. (2022) *Representation Matters*. London: Bloomsbury.

Vandello, J.A. & Cohen, D. (2003) Male honor and female fidelity: Implicit cultural scripts that perpetuate domestic violence. *Journal of Personality and Social Psychology*, 84(5), 997–1010.

Wheeler, S. (ed.) (2006) *Difference and Diversity in Counselling*. Basingstoke: Palgrave Macmillan.

Winer, C. (2021) The trouble with 'intersectional identities'. *Academia Letters*, Article 819. https://doi.org/10.20935/AL819.

Appendix

1. Identity Wheel (with Identity Characteristics) tool
2. Identity Wheel tool (template)
3. Scales of Power in Identity Characteristics tool (template)
4. Scales of Power in Identity Characteristics in Counselling tool (template)
5. Scales of Relational Power tool (template)
6. Anti-Oppressive Self-Care Wheel tool (template)

Additional copies of these five resources can be downloaded and printed from-https://library.jkp.com/redeem using the password code FTHRMFA.

Identity Wheel (with Identity Characteristics) tool

Identity Wheel tool (template)

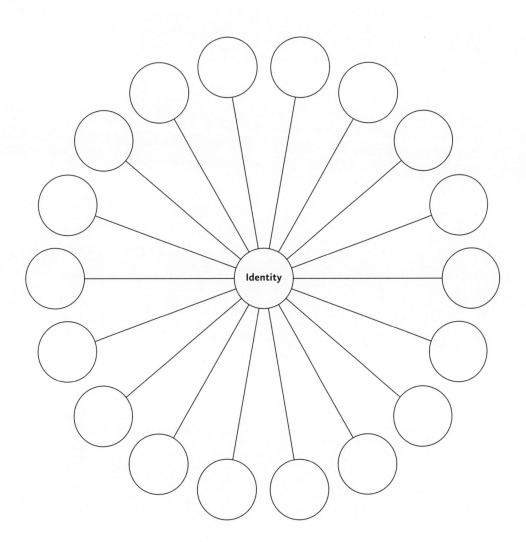

Scales of Power in Identity Characteristics tool (template)

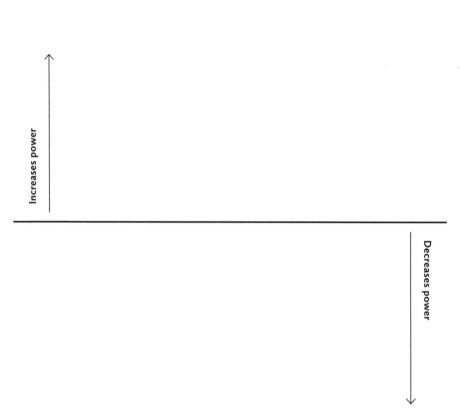

Increases power

Decreases power

Scales of Power in Identity Characteristics in Counselling tool (template)

Being:
Counsellor

Increases power

Being:
Client

Decreases power

Scales of Relational Power tool (template)

Increases power

↑ *Counsellor's privileged identities:*

↑ *Client's privileged identities:*

Counsellor's oppressed identities:

Client's oppressed identities:

Decreases power

Anti-Oppressive Self-Care Wheel tool (template)

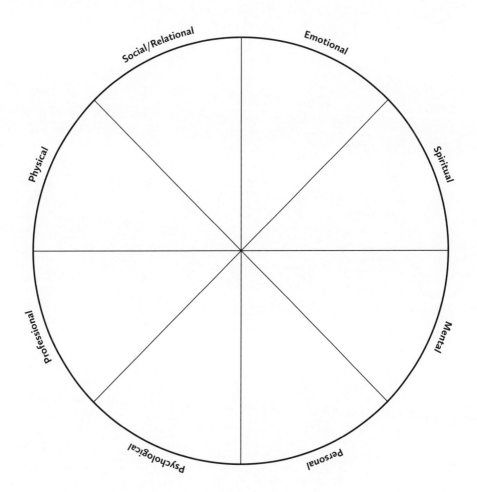